BIBLIOTHECA MESOPOTAMICA

Volume Two

Part One

Bibliotheca Mesopotamica

Primary sources and interpretive analyses for the study of Mesopotamian civilization and its influences from late prehistory to the end of the cuneiform tradition

Edited by Giorgio Buccellati

Volume Two, Fascicle One

Babylonian Planetary Omens: Part One

The Venus Tablet of Ammiṣaduqa

by Erica Reiner
in collaboration with David Pingree

Undena Publications
Malibu 1975

BABYLONIAN PLANETARY OMENS

PART ONE

ENŪMA ANU ENLIL
TABLET 63:
THE VENUS TABLET OF AMMIṢADUQA

by

Erica Reiner

in collaboration with

David Pingree

UNDENA PUBLICATIONS
MALIBU, 1975

This edition of Enuma Anu Enlil is dedicated to the memory of A. Leo Oppenheim. He inspired both of us in many ways, and initiated and fostered our collaboration on Babylonian astral omens.

Undena Publications, P.O. Box 97, Malibu, Calif. 90265

Library of Congress Card Number: 75-26241 *Reprinted July 2000*

ISBN: 0-89003-010-3

CONTENTS

FOREWORD

Enūma Anu Enlil (EAE) is the name by which the series of celestial omens was known to the Babylonians. The name, as usual, is taken from the first words of the series' incipit. Scholars engaged in compiling, copying, and annotating the series were each called *tupšar Enūma Anu Enlil*, "scribe of Enūma Anu Anlil," and so, eventually, were the astronomers of Seleucid Babylonia.[1] The canonical corpus of celestial omens was divided by these scribes into about 70 tablets. The first fifty, dealing with the moon, the sun, and meteorological phenomena, were organized—but not edited—by E. Weidner,[2] from the cuneiform texts in the British Museum published by Ch. Virolleaud in autograph copies, with transliterations but without translation, from 1908 to 1912,[3] and from texts in other museums.

The last twenty-odd tablets contain omens derived from the movements of the planets and the stars, and for these not even a preliminary organization exists. It is, however, precisely these omens that are most significant for students of the history of science.

Therefore, at the suggestion of Professors Neugebauer and Sachs, we are beginning the publication of the series EAE with the tablets that contain the planetary omens, that is, Tablets 50 and following, in a series of fascicles. Each fascicle will contain one or more tablets whose serial number is known, or, failing this, whose subject matter can be subsumed under some general heading. All fragments known to be part of the canonical series will be used to reconstruct the text; other fragments and scholia will appear as appendices to the canonical text. Each fascicle will also contain a glossary of technical terms (except for the present fascicle) and a list of apodoses.

First to be published is the present edition of Tablet 63, the "Venus Tablet." It is presented first because of its intrinsic interest for historians concerned with the chronology of the First Babylonian Dynasty, and also for the practical reason that it presents the fewest philological problems in its reconstruction (no overlap with any other tablet of EAE is possible) and its terminology (see Introduction p. 7). It will be followed by the edition of Tablets 50-52. Texts not previously published in autograph copy will be presented in the form of photographs on microfiche, as soon as enough photographs accumulate to fill such a microfiche.

The various fascicles containing one or more tablets of the series will be published as parts of individual volumes of the series *Bibliotheca Mesopotamica*. To facilitate the eventual use of the volumes as complete units, page numeration according to volume is given in square brackets at the bottom of each page—e.g. [*BM* 2,1] meaning volume 2 of *BM* page 1. A separate title page and table of contents will be provided upon completion of each volume.

It is a pleasure to acknowledge a grant from the John Simon Guggenheim Memorial Foundation for this project, which made possible collations of tablets in the British Museum.

The contributions of each author will be identified when these can be separated conveniently. In most cases, however, the textual interpretation relies on knowledge of both astronomy and of the texts pertaining to the history of astronomy that David Pingree is providing. This collaboration should result eventually not only in the edition of the Babylonian corpus, but also in a critical evaluation of it for the history of astronomy.

1. A. L. Oppenheim, "Divination and Celestial Observation in the Last Assyrian Empire," *Centaurus* 14 (1969), 99f.; O. Neugebauer, *Astronomical Cuneiform Texts* (London, 1955) 13f.
2. E. Weidner, "Die astrologische Serie Enūma Anu Enlil," *Archiv für Orientforschung* 14 (1941-1944), 172-195, 308-318; ibid. 17 (1954-1956), 71-89; ibid. 22 (1968-1969) 65-75.
3. Ch. Virolleaud, *L'Astrologie Chaldéenne, Le Livre intitulé "enuma (Anu* ^{ilu}*Bêl*," fascicles 1-8 (Paris, 1908-1909); idem, *Supplément* (Paris, 1910); *Second Supplément* (Paris, 1912).

PHILOLOGICAL INTRODUCTION

The sources for Tablet 63 of the Series *Enūma Anu Enlil,*[1] the so-called Venus Tablets of Ammiṣaduqa, have been increased from the seven known to Langdon and Fotheringham[2] to twenty. With the exception of one text (from Assur?) in the Staatliche Museen (Berlin), published by René Labat, MIO 5 322 and pl. xix (=p. 344), and identified by me as a "Venus Tablet," all new sources are from the collections of the British Museum. Three fragments (E, K, N; see Table Ia) were previously published in LBAT, and identified by A. Sachs in the introductory catalogue to that volume. The others have been identified by me upon inspection of the omen fragments characterized as "astrological" in Bezold's *Catalogue of the Cuneiform Tablets in the Kouyunjik Collection of the British Museum* and from the list of *Enūma Anu Enlil* type material in the British Museum, compiled and generously put at my disposal by A. Sachs. Therefore, it is eminently possible that further fragments may come to light among unpublished texts in other museums, and even in the British Museum itself. This fact is stressed here because, as will become clear from the presentation of the material, all but one of the twenty pieces present the material in such a uniform way that probably no more than two recensions–alike but for the fact that one includes omens 38-59, and the other omits them and adds an extra omen (60)–have to be reconstructed from these late manuscripts, even though the history of the canonical recension may be a complex one, as set forth by David Pingree on pp. 15 ff.

The fifty-nine omens of this tablet, as noted by previous editors and commentators,[2] fall into four sections. Sections I (omens 1-21) and III (omens 34-37) deal with pairs of last and first visibilities of Venus; they are separated by section II (omens 22-33). Most of the omens in I and III are repeated in IV (omens 38-59) wherein they are rearranged in the order of the months. Section II also was excerpted in the series *Iqqur īpuš* where it more properly belongs; see p. 10.

On the assumption that several fragments, though not direct joins, belong to the same tablet (A and M; F and H; L, P, and Q; T and U), the number of exemplars attested may be reduced from twenty to fifteen. Although none of the sources is completely preserved, certain conclusions can be drawn about the content and arrangement of the various exemplars (see Table Ib).

1. All four sections I-IV were contained in exemplar A (+) M and probably in J. If L (+) P (+) Q are parts of one tablet, that exemplar contained sections II-IV, and hence probably I-IV; if G belongs to the same tablet, it certainly contained I-IV.
2. Sections I-III only were contained in C.
3. Sections I-III, plus omen 60, were contained in B, and probably also in R and N. In N, only III and omen 60 are preserved; in R, the subscript preceding omen 60 and omen 60.
4. Exemplar T (+) U contained only section IV, and may represent the second tablet of a recension in which I-IV were written on two tablets, and therefore may be the continuation of an exemplar such as C (or of C itself).

---

[1] The number 63 is based on one system of numbering; in another system of serialization, the number 63 is given to the tablet we shall call 64.

[2] See Bibliography.

5. The other sources are so fragmentary that it cannot be established whether they belong to one of the two basic type exemplars, namely manuscript tradition x–above (1) and possibly above (2) plus (4)– and y–above (3). Sections I and II are attested in F (+) H and probably D; only section I in G; only IV in K, O, and V; only II in L which, therefore, may belong to *Iqqur īpuš* (see below).

6. The placement of K is not certain; E cannot be placed, and is given in separate transliteration on p. 64.

Note that V (an Assur text?) is the only manuscript which uses MUL *Dil-bat* for Venus instead of Ninsianna (all other manuscripts).

Each section is delimited not only by its content and, for section IV, also its form, but by a subscript. We have identified eight subscripts, S_1–S_8, though some of these may have to be collapsed.

The first subscript, S_1, occurs after section I; unfortunately, it is illegible in C, and in H–which sets off this section from the next by a double ruling–only the middle portion of the subscript line is preserved, and this portion is blank, so that the nature of S_1 is unknown. (However, in C at least, the subscript was not of the form *n kiṣrū,* because the traces do not allow such an interpretation.)

S_2, the subscript after omen 33, is attested in B, C, D, (A +) M, and N, and reads as follows: *12 kiṣrū tāmurātu*[3] *ša Ninsianna* GABA.RI *Bābili* 'twelve omens, visibilities[3] of Venus, copy of (a text from) Babylon'.

Section III is followed in C by a subscript S_3 which may represent the subscript to Tablet 63; of it only the end, [. . .] *kî pî labīrišu* '[. . .] according to its original', is preserved. In N, a subscript of two lines, S_4, occurs; the first line is fragmentary and what is preserved is not intelligible; the second line in its preserved part has [. . .] TA *kiṣri* '[. . .] from the omen(s)'. A subscript in both P and K, that we call S_5, preceded the next section, IV; what preceded it is not preserved in P, and cannot be identified as omen 37 in K. Probably it is to be restored as [*4 kiṣrū ša*] *Ninsianna aḫûtu* 'four extraneous omens about Venus'; in P, only the word *Ninsianna* is preserved.

S_6, the subscript that concludes Tablet 63 in A and J, is identical in its preserved portion to S_5, and is probably to be restored as [*21 kiṣrū ša*] *Ninsianna aḫûtu.* In R, only the second half of the subscript is preserved: [. . . *kiṣ*]*ri tajārta ina libbi išû;* this subscript, S_7, may be restored from S_8; see below, and the interpretation proposed on p. 9. In B, this subscript takes up two lines, but the first line is broken with the exception of the first two signs. The second sign may be *ki*, permitting a restoration *ki*[*ṣru*]; the first sign is partly broken, and if it is a numeral it can be only the figure 4. Therefore, we have concluded that this subscript is probably identical with S_4 and S_5, and that manuscripts B and R, and probably N, did not contain section IV.

The additional omen 60 that follows S_7 in B and R, and probably also in N, is a repetition of omen 17 (also appearing as omen 50 in section IV), but correcting the erroneous eastern setting of omen 17 to a western setting.

This omen is again followed by a subscript in B and R, S_8. S_8 is better preserved than S_7, and may be used for the restoration of S_7: *2 kiṣrū ša Ninsianna aḫûtu ultu libbi kiṣri tajārātu ina libbi išû.* Its beginning is preserved only in B, and the figure 2 is beyond doubt, in spite of the fact that the section preceding S_8 (the section between S_7 and S_8) contains only one omen, not two.

---

[3]Collation shows a clear *-mu-* as the second sign in this word, thus excluding the reading TA *gaba-ra-tum* retained by Labat, Calendrier p. 199, in spite of the objections of Langdon, The Venus Tablets, p. 13 note 1. It is assumed here that *tāmurātu* is a variant of *tāmarātu,* although such a variant form is not attested elsewhere, because the twelve omens preceding refer to risings (IGI.DU_8 = *tāmartu*) of Venus. Professor Borger (orally) suggested that the sign MU may stand for ia_5 so that this subscript too would contain the term *tajārātu,* for which see note 5.

Subscripts S_7 and S_8 employ a terminology not otherwise attested, and their interpretation is uncertain. They may be translated: ‘n extraneous omens about Venus, from an omen (or: the omens); they have returns therein’. The word translated as ‘omen’ is *kiṣru;* it was translated as ‘section (of a text)’ in CAD K 441a sub 8a, but the references cited there could also be interpreted as ‘omens’; the translation ‘omens’ is chosen here because the subscript to the twelve omens of section II uses the same term.

The word translated as ‘return’ is *tajārtu* (plural: *tajārātu*). It is normally used (in the singular) for the ‘return (march)’ from a campaign in Neo-Assyrian annals and, in transferred meaning, for ‘pardon’;[4] only a few atypical occurrences[5] suggest the meaning ‘repetition’ that seems to be required in the subscripts.

Source B also gives the total number of omens on the tablet in the colophon. The number, slightly broken, may be either 34 or 37. The number 34 would account for the total of sections I and II (21 + 12) and the added omen 60; the number 37 would account for all omens of sections I, II, and III (21 + 12 + 4).

The basis for the attribution of the eight-year cycles of Venus of Tablet 63 to the reign of Ammiṣaduqa, and specifically of the first such cycle (omens 1-10) to a Venus-cycle in the first eight years of his reign, is of course the name of year 8 of Ammiṣaduqa[6] that follows the first ten omens. However, the tenth omen, the last of the cycle, is incomplete. In fact, it consists solely of the statement ‘Venus disappeared in the east on the 25th of month XII’. Thus, it is not an omen, because it lacks an apodosis; moreover, it also differs from omens 1-9 (and 11-20 of the “second cycle”) because it lacks the period of invisibility and the date of the next first visibility. The date of the disappearance of Venus is stated as an event. We know that ominous occurrences that were observed in an extispicy, namely markings and features on the liver and lungs of the lamb, were reported in the Old Babylonian period.[7] All those reports that are dated date to the reigns of the last two kings of the First Dynasty of Babylon, Ammiṣaduqa (fourteen reports) and Samsuditana (two).[8] It is therefore our belief that omen 10 was not shortened from a complete omen in order to find space for the name of the year, but that it was originally a report of an observation of the last visibility of Venus, followed by the date, as in the case of the reports of haruspices.

It should be noted that the fragmentary line [. . .] KÙ.GI. g a . k e$_4$, that is, the end of the year name of Ammiṣaduqa 8, occurs on another fragment of celestial omens, Sm. 1057:8'.

With the exception of omen 10, the omens of sections I, III, and IV, and omen 60 all follow the same pattern: In month MN, day n, Venus disappeared in the east/west; it remains invisible for n days, and became visible in month MN_2, day n, in the west/east: apodosis. While the verbs *itbal* ‘disappeared’ and *innamir* ‘became visible’ may be in the past tense because of the general style of omens, according to which the introductory *šumma* (‘if’) governs a grammatical preterite, it is to be noted that the verb ‘remains invisible’ nonetheless is in the present tense—*uḫḫaram(-ma)*—in all sources which use a syllabic spelling in

---

[4]Note that in CT 28 29 r. 6 *ta-a-a-ár-tum* is not a gloss, as assumed in Kraus Texte 33 Index s.v., but is the apodosis, ‘pardon’, of the omen.

[5]These atypical occurrences are of three types:

a) referring to a feature or deformation of the gall bladder observed in extispicy: *šumma martum ta-a-a-ra-tim išû* YOS 10 31 iv 7-9; *šumma martu imitta u šumēla ta-a-a-ra-ti itaddât(*ŠUB.MEŠ-*át)* CT 28 48 K.182 + r. 7.

b) rubric at the end of a bilingual incantation: [*t*]*a-a-a-ár-ti ša* ÉN AGA.MAḪ [*t*]*u-qat-te-e-ma* ŠID-*n*[*u*] ‘you recite to the end the *tajārtu* of the incantation “AGA.MAḪ”’ K.5246:7f. (courtesy R. Borger).

c) in EAE fragments: [. . . *ta-a-a-á*]*r-tu i-šu-ú* DÙ-*ma* (=*kalama*) *šá* E-[*ú* . . .] (=*ša iqbû*) ^{d}UDU.IDIM.MEŠ DÙ-*ma* (=*kalama*) *ana* ^{d}UTU.ŠÚ.A *ta-a-a-ár-tú ir-*[*šu-ú*] (commentary on [DIŠ MUL.MEŠ *ana*] ^{d}UTU.È *nap-ḫu-ni* ‘if the stars rise toward east’) Rm. 932:4'-6', cf. (in broken context) [. . . *ta-a-a-ú*]*r-tum i-šu-u ka-la-ma la ka-l*[*a-ma* . . .] ibid. 3'.

[6]See Ungnad, RlA 2 190 no. 256.

[7]For a convenient survey, see Goetze, YOS 10 pp. 2 and 4, and JCS 11 89ff., also Nougayrol, JCS 21 219ff.

[8]Nougayrol, JCS 21 220 n. 3.

sections I and III and in omen 60, but in the preterite–*uḫḫiram(-ma)*–in section IV. The logographic spelling ZAL may represent either the preterite *uḫḫiram(-ma)* or the present *uḫḫaram(-ma)*.

The omens of section II follow a different pattern: they begin not with the disappearance, but with the appearance of Venus. After the introductory 'In MN, day n, Venus appeared in the east/west', there follows A(podosis)$_1$. Then comes an amplification or explanation: 'It remains present in the east/west until month MN$_2$, day n; it disappears in MN$_2$, day n+1, and remains invisible for three months/seven days; in MN$_3$, day n (= MN$_2$, day n+1 plus three months or seven days), it rises in the west/east: A(podosis)$_2$'. The second section may be called an amplification or explanation because the verb forms in this section are always in the present, and are all followed by the particle *-ma*. This verb form is characteristic of the explanations given in commented texts. Commented texts are of the pattern protasis - apodosis - commentary, and this is the pattern found in the omens of section II, with the difference only that in these omens a second apodosis follows. Not only is it unique that two apodoses occur in two different parts of an omen; the two apodoses are dissimilar, and sometimes contradictory–an occurrence found, to be sure, in other omen series, but with the specification that the second apodosis (which always immediately follows the first) is a variant from another source.

The structure of these omens of section II, and their relation to Tablet 63, remains unique. As mentioned briefly on p. 3 , this section was excerpted in at least some recensions of the series *Iqqur īpuš*,[9] a series deriving omens from various activities undertaken by a person (in some recensions by the king) in the twelve months of the year, with the day of the month remaining unspecified.[10] Some tablets of *Iqqur īpuš* which are organized by months (Labat's *Séries Mensuelles*) list as the last of the omens derived from celestial phenomena–moon, sun, Venus, meteorological and atmospheric phenomena–an omen from the rising of Venus which is one of omens 22-33. (For months I, III, IX, and X see Labat, Calendrier p. 199; for month VI, ibid. p. 259.) A further, unpublished, fragment of such a monthly section of *Iqqur īpuš* for month II, K. 7939, also contains the omen from Venus' rising (= EAE 63 omen 23); it is possible that sources for the other months also contained this omen. However, in the first part of *Iqqur īpuš*, in which a paragraph is devoted to each activity, no separate paragraph for the risings of Venus through the twelve months has so far been attested, but such a paragraph was included by Labat as § 104A of *Iqqur īpuš* because of the occurrence of such omens in the monthly series. One of the texts which at first was taken to belong to Tablet 63, K.3170 + 11719 + 14551, turned out to be part of *Iqqur īpuš*, because, while it has omens 22-27 on the reverse, it has other *Iqqur īpuš* paragraphs on the obverse. The pertinent omens from this text are edited in Appendix A. Source L of Tablet 63, K.12344 + 12758, with omens 25-29, may also be part of *Iqqur īpuš* rather than of Tablet 63.

This fact raises anew the question posed by Labat, op. cit. pp. 9f., whether *Iqqur īpuš* borrowed from other omen series, or vice versa. As far as planetary omens are concerned, Labat included five paragraphs on Venus (§§ 82-86), and on pp. 170f. note 6 mentions the possibility that two paragraphs concerning Jupiter and one concerning ^{d}UDU.IDIM of EAE may have been incorporated in some editions of *Iqqur īpuš*. Without attempting to solve the general problem of the relationship of *Iqqur īpuš* to other omen texts, we would point out that section II of EAE 63 (omens 22-33) fits into the monthly schema which forms the structure of *Iqqur īpuš*. Section IV, in which omens 1-21 and 34-37 are rearranged in the order of the months, does not fit into the schema of *Iqqur īpuš* because most months occur more than once in the sequence.

[9] Edited by René Labat, *Un Calendrier babylonien des travaux, des signes, et des mois (Séries* Iqqur īpuš) (Paris, 1965).

[10] §§ 41' and 66' form an exception; they refer to any month of the year, with the day of the month–from 1 to 30–being the variable.

Table Ia. Sources.

A	K.2321 + 3032	Neobabylonian. AAT 46; ACh Ištar 12, 15; Langdon-Fotheringham pl. 5-6. Omens 1-14; break; 45-59; S_6; end (colophon).
B	W 1924.802	Neobabylonian. Langdon-Fotheringham pl. 3-4. Omens 1-11; break; S_2; 34-37; S_7; 60; S_8; end (colophon). Found at Kish in 1924.
C	K.160	3R 63; ACh Ištar 12-14; Langdon-Fotheringham pl. 1-2. Photo: ACh frontispiece. Omens 8-21; S_1; 22-33; S_2; 34-37; S_3; break.
D	K.7225	Photo. Column i: omens 7-12; break. Column ii: broken, possibly S_2.
E	BM 41498	Neobabylonian. LBAT 1562. See Appendix B.
F	BM 37010	Neobabylonian. Omens 12-15; break.
G	Rm. 2,531	Langdon-Fotheringham pl. 3. Omens 15-20; break.
H	BM 36758 + 37496	Neobabylonian. Photo of BM 36758. Omens 19-21; S_1; 22-27; break.
J	BM 36395	Neobabylonian. Photo. Omens 3-15; break; 54-59; S_6; end (colophon).
K	BM 34227 + 42033	Neobabylonian. LBAT 1561 + 1560. Two unidentified omens (see Appendix C); S_5; omens 38-42; break.
L	K.12344 + 12758	Omens 25-29; break.
M	K.3105	Neobabylonian. Photo. Omens 27-33; S_2; 34-36; break.
N	BM 41688	Neobabylonian. LBAT 1563. S_2; omens 34-37; S_4; $60^?$; break.
O	BM 37121 + 37432	Neobabylonian. Omens 53-56; break.
P	K.7072	ACh Supp. 42. S_5; omens 38-40; break.
Q	Sm. 174	Babyloniaca 3 285; Langdon-Fotheringham pl. 6. Omens 45-48; break.
R	K.7090	Photo. S_7; 60; S_8; end (colophon).
T	K.5963 + Rm. 134	ACh Supp. 41 (Rm. 134 only). Omens 38-41; break.
U	K.12186	Omens 56-58; break.
V	VAT 11253	MIO 5 pl. 19 (= p. 344). Omens 41-45; break; 57-59; break.

A and M may be parts of the same tablet.

F and H may be parts of the same tablet.

L, P, and Q may be parts of the same tablet.

T and U may be parts of the same tablet.

V has been collated by Dr. Liane Jakob-Rost. All other sources have been collated by E. Reiner; in addition, numbers on all British Museum tablets (i.e., all sources except B and V) have also been checked by Asgar Aaboe.

Table Ib. Arrangement of Sources According to Manuscript Traditions.

Manuscript Families	Sources	Sections										
		I		II		III		IV				
x	A (+) M	1 - (21);		(22) - 33;	S_2;	34 - (37);	[ ]	(38) - 59;	S_6;	—	—	—
	J	(1) - (21);	[				]	(38) - 59;	S_6;	—	—	—
	(G +)L (+) P(+)Q	(1) - (21);		(22) - (33);	[	]	S_5;	38 - (59);	[			
	K	[				] ?	S_5;	38 - (59)				
y	B	1 - (21);	[	]	S_2;	34 - 37	—	—	—	S_7;	60;	S_8
	R	[							]	S_7;	60;	S_8
	N	[		]	S_2;	34 - 37;	S_4;	—	—	—	60;	[
z	C	(1) - 21;	S_1;	22 - 33	S_2;	34 - 37;	S_3	—	—	—	—	—
	(+) T + U							38 - (59)	[			

Note. Parentheses around the first or last number in the columns under sections I-IV indicate that the first or last omens of the section are not preserved, but the section is attested in the manuscript through some of the omens.

Table II. Apodoses.

The following is a list of the apodoses attested in Tablet 63. They are arranged in alphabetical order, and followed by the serial number of the omen or omens to which they belong. The letters *a* and *b* after numbers 22-33 refer to A_1 and A_2 of these omens respectively.

1.	*ebūr māti iššir* 'the harvest of the land will prosper'	2, 6, 12, 15, 30b, 31a, 32ab, [41], 52, 53, 54, 55
2.	*ebūr māti iššir libbi māti iṭâb* (= 1 + 6)	23b, 27a, 28b, 31b
3.	*ebūr ruṭibti iššir libbi māti iṭâb* 'the harvest of the irrigated land will prosper, the land will be happy'	21
4.	*ḫušaḫḫi še'i u tibni ina māti ibašši* 'there will be scarcity of barley and straw in the land'	30a
5.	*ḫušaḫḫi še'i u tibni ina māti ibašši ubbutu iššakkan* 'there will be scarcity of barley and straw in the land, there will be . . . '[11]	7, 51
6.	*libbi māti iṭâb* 'the land will be happy'	4, 13, 14, 35, [38], [42], 49
7.	*māta dannatu iṣabbat* 'hard times will befall the land'	29a, 33b
8.	*mātu ana dannati ipaḫḫur* 'the land will assemble in the fortresses'	30b variant from *Iqqur īpuš*
9.	*mērešu iššir* 'the arable land will prosper'	34 variant
10.	*miqitti ummāni matti* 'downfall of a large army'	24a, 58
11.	*miqitti ummān-manda: miqitti* [. . .] 'downfall of the Manda-troops, variant: downfall of [a large army?]'	20
12.	MU SAL *ina māti rūqti ibašši: ina* É.GAL GU.LA 'there will be . . . in a distant land, variant: in the large? palace'	34
13.	*nagbū ippaṭṭaru Adad zunnēšu Ea nagbēšu ubbala šarru ana šarri salīma išappar* 'springs will open? , Adad will bring his rains, Ea his floods, king will send messages of reconciliation to king'	1, 57 (omitting *nagbū ippaṭṭaru*)
14.	*nukurātu ina māti ibaššâ* 'there will be hostilities in the land'	23a, 24b, 25a, 27b
15.	*nukurātu ina māti ibaššâ ebūru iššir* 'there will be hostilities in the land, the harvest will prosper'	3, 48
16.	*nukurātu ina māti ibaššâ ebūr māti iššir* (= 14 + 1)	26b, 28a, 29b, 36, 39
17.	*ruṭibtu iššir libbi māti iṭâb* (cf. 3)	59 second part
18.	*šarrāni* [. . .] 'kings [. . .]'	33a
19.	*šarru ana šarri nukurta išappar* 'king will send messages of hostility to king'	22b, 25b
20.	*šarru ana šarri salīma išappar* 'king will send messages of reconciliation to king'	11, 21 variant, 59 first part

[11] The reading *ubbutu* has been chosen instead of *arbūtu*, partly because the apodoses differ from those in which *arbūtu* occurs, and partly because the spelling *ub-bu-tu* occurs on an unpublished Old Babylonian tablet of EAE in a similar apodosis. The spelling *ub-bu-tu* may stand for *ubbuṭu* 'famine', while *ubbutu* is explained by *šalputtu* 'desecration' in Izbu Comm. 94.

21.	*šarru ana šarri ṣalta išappar* 'king will send messages of war to king'	11 variant, 37, 56
22.	*urubātu ina māti ibaššâ* 'there will be mourning in the land'	22a
23.	*zunnū ina māti ibaššû ubbutu iššakkan* 'there will be rains in the land, there will be . . . '	8, 9, 17, 18, 46, 47, 50, 60
24.	*zunnū ina šamê ibaššû ubbutu ibašši* 'there will be rains from the sky, there will be . . . '	26a
25.	*zunnū ina šamê mīlū ina nagbī ibaššû* 'there will be rains from the sky, floods from the springs'	19
26.	*zunnū ina šamê* [. . .] *ebūr māti iššir* (= 19? + 1)	45
27.	*zunnū u mīlū ibaššû ebūr māti iššir* 'there will be rains and floods, the harvest of the land will prosper'	5, 40

THE ASTRONOMICAL AND TEXTUAL PROBLEMS

(By David Pingree)

Astronomical Data in the Protases of Omens 1-21, 34-37, and 38-60.

In one synodic period of approximately 584 days the planet Venus makes one rotation about the Sun. (See Figure 1 for a sketch of the orbits of Venus and of the Earth around the Sun). If we consider a rotation to begin with the planet's last visibility in the East (Σ), it will then be approaching superior conjunction with the Sun and its furthest distance from the Earth. Between last visibility in the East (Σ) and first visibility in the West (Ξ) it will be invisible for two months and some days. After its first visibility in the West it remains visible for eight months and some days before its last visibility in the West (Ω) occurs, and it approaches inferior conjunction with the Sun. It remains invisible for as little as three days in the winter, for as much as two weeks and a few days in the summer, before its first visibility in the East (Γ) occurs. Then it is again visible for eight months and some days before its last visibility in the East (Σ). Of course, observations of "last visibilities" can occur before the expected dates and those of "first visibilities" after the expected dates; but *if a watch were kept every night*, such variations because of observational difficulties should not have expanded the periods of invisibility or contracted those of visibility by more than a few days.

As has been pointed out in the introduction, the text consists of four sections, of which section IV is a monthly rearrangement of sections I and III; omen 60 is a corrected form of omen 17. The identifications of these omens are given in Table III.

Table III. Correlations of Omens 38-60 with 1-21 and 34-37.

Note. The number on the left refers to the omens in section IV, the number on the right to the omens in sections I and III. Where the identification is confirmed by the preserved apodoses (see Table II), an asterisk is added.

*38 = 14	44 = 9	*50 = 17	*56 = 37
*39 = 36	*45 = 19	*51 = 7	*57 = 1
*40 = 5	*46 = 8	*52 = 2	*58 = 20
*41 = 15	*47 = 18	*53 = 12	*59 = 21
*42 = 35	*48 = 3	*54 = 6	*60 = 17
43 = 4	*49 = 13	55 = 16	

Figure 1. The Orbits of Venus and the Earth

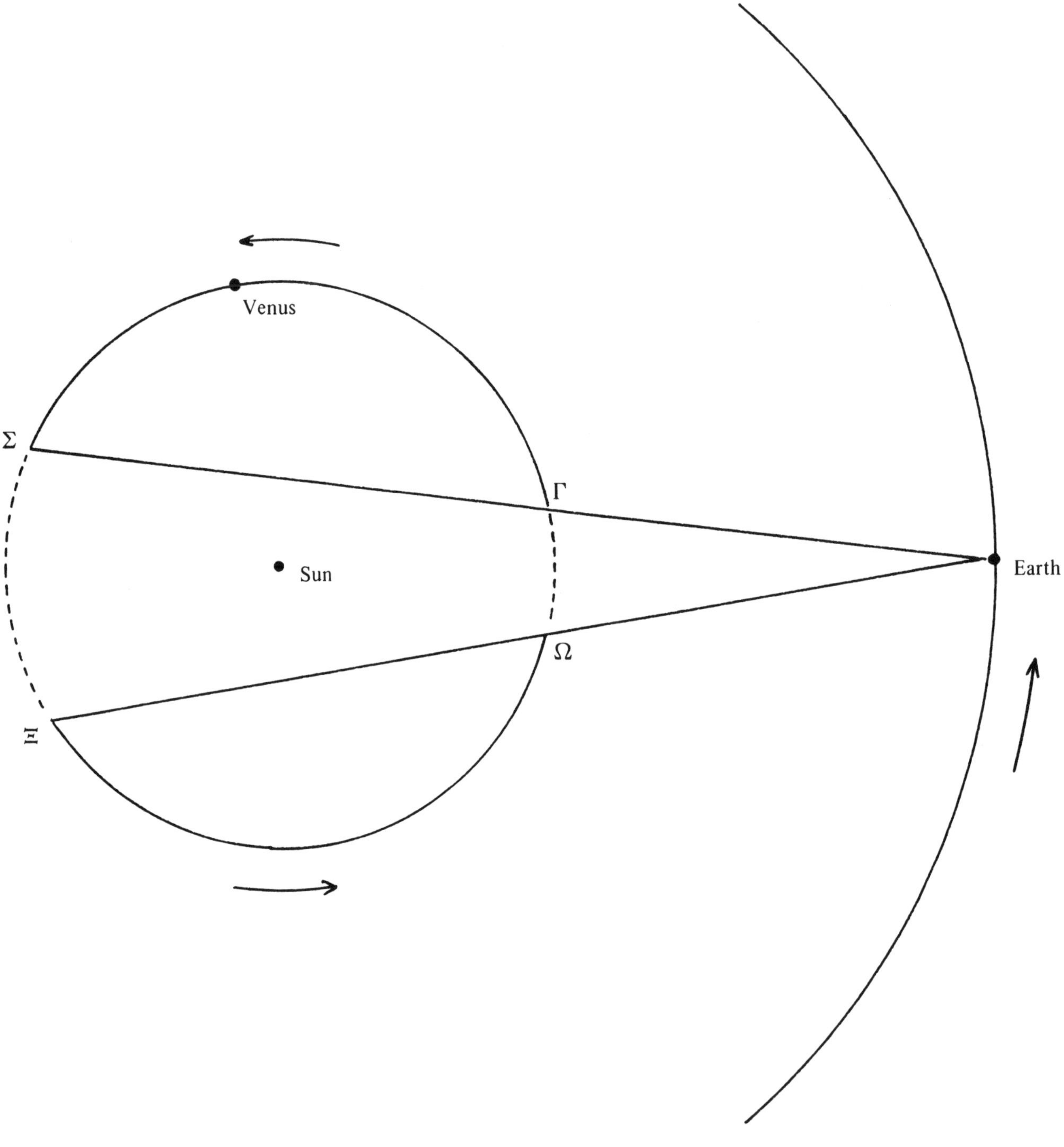

Note. This diagram is not drawn to scale. The actual dates and longitudes of the phenomena of Venus depend on variables not represented in this simplified scheme.

In table IV are given the dates and periods of invisibility from each omen in sections I and III and from the corresponding omens in section IV and omen 60. The copies preserving the information are indicated in parentheses. A column is added indicating the intervals of visibility computed on the assumption also made by the scribe who computed the periods of invisibility recorded in the text—that is, that each month contains 30 days. In the margin is given in square brackets the number of the regnal year of Ammiṣaduqa in which the last visibility of each omen would have fallen on the assumption that sections I and III contain observations of the 21 years of his reign.

Table IV. The Astronomical Data in the Order of Omens 1-21.

Year	Omens	Last visibility	Interval of invisibility	First visibility	Interval of visibility
[1]	1	Ω XI 15 (B)	3d (AB)	Γ XI 18 (B)	8m 23d (B)
		Ω (A)		Γ (A)	
	57	Ω (AU)	3d (AJ)	Γ XI 18 (J)	
				XI 18 (U)	
				XI 28 (A)	
[2]	2	Σ VIII 11 (B)	2m 7d (B)	Ξ X 19 (B)	8m 4d (B)
		Σ (A)	2m 8d (A)	Ξ (A)	
	52	Σ (A)	2m 8d (A)	Ξ X 19 (A)	
[3]	3	Ω VI 23 (B)	20d (AB)	Γ VII 13 (B)	8m 19d (B)
		Ω (A)		Γ (A)	
	48	Ω VI 23 (A)	20d (A)	Γ VII 13 (A)	
		Ω (Q)			
[4]	4	Σ VII[1] 2 (B)	2m 1d (AB)	Ξ VI 3 (B)	8[2]m 29d (B)
		Σ (A)		VI 3 (J)	
				Ξ (A)	
	43				
[5]	5	Ω II 2 (B)	18d (B)	Γ II 18 (B)	8[3]m 7d (B)
		Ω (A)	15d (A)	II (AJ)	
	40	Ω II 2 (KP)	*x* d (P)	Γ II 28 or 18 (K)	
		II 2 (T)		Γ (T)	

[1]A scribal error for IV.

[2]Including the attested XII_2 in Ammiṣaduqa 4.

[3]Including the alleged VI_2 in Ammiṣaduqa 5.

(Table IV continued)

Year	Omens	Last visibility	Interval of invisibility	First visibility	Interval of visibility
[5]	6	Σ IX 25 (B)	2m 4d (AB)	Ξ XI 29 (B)	8m 29d (B)
		Σ IX 12 (A)		Ξ XI 16 (A)	
			4d (J)	XI 28 (J)	
	54	Σ *x* + 1 (A)	2m *x*d (AO)	Ξ (AO)	
		Σ 12 (O)			
[6]	7	Ω VIII 18[4] (B)	3d (AB)	Γ IX 1 (B)	8m 20d (B + A)
		VIII 20 + *x* (A)		IX 1 (A)	
				IX (J)	
	51	Ω VIII 28 (A)	5d (A)	Γ IX (A)	
[7]	8	Σ V 21 (A)	2m 11d (B)	Ξ VIII 2 (A)	8m 23d (AC)
		Σ (BC)	*x*m *x* + 1d (A)	VIII 2 (C)	
				VIII (J)	
	46	Σ (Q)		Ξ (Q)	
[8]	9	Ω IV 25 (AC)	7d (BCD)	Γ V 2 (ACJ)	7$^{!}$ m 23d (AC)
				Γ (D)	
	44	IV (V)		Ξ$^{!}$ (Q)	
				IV (V)	
[8]	10	Σ XII 25 (AC)			
[9]	11	Ω III 11 (AC)	9m 4d (CD)	Γ XII 15 (AC)	8[5]m 25d (C)
			9m *x*d (A)	Γ (D)	
			*x*m 5d (J)	XII 16 (J)	
[10]	12	Σ VIII 10 (AC)	2m 6d (C)	Ξ X 16 (ACJ)	8m 10d (C)
			*x*m 6d (D)		
			2m 16$^{?}$ d (F)		
	53	Σ (O)	2m 8d (A)	Ξ X 16 (A)	
			2m *x*d (O)	Ξ (O)	

[4] A scribal error for 28.

[5] Including the attested VI_2 in Ammiṣaduqa 10.

(Table IV continued)

Year	Omens	Last visibility	Interval of invisibility	First visibility	Interval of visibility
[11]	13	Ω VI 26 (C)	11d (CF)	Γ VI$_2$[6] 7 (CJ)	7$^!$ m 2d (C)
	49	Ω VI 26 (A)	12d (A)	Γ VI$_2$ 8 (A)	
[12]	14	Σ I 9 (C)	5m 16d (CF)	Ξ VI 25 (CJ)	7$^!$ m 10d (C)
	38	Σ I 8 (K)	5m 18d (K)	VI *x* (K)	
		I 8 (T)	5m 17d (T)	VI 25 (T)	
		I (P)		VI 24 (P)	
[13]	15	Ω II 5 (C)	7d (CFG)	Γ *x* + 1 (F)	8m 9d (FG + G)
				Γ (CJ)	
				12 (G)	
	41	Ω II 5 (K)	7d (T)	Γ (KT)	
		5 (T)	6d$^!$ (V)	III (V)	
[13]	16	Σ X 20 (C)	15d (C)	Ξ XI 11 (CG)	8[7]m 29d (CG)
		X 21 (G)		Ξ (J)	
	55	Ω$^!$ 24 (O)	1m *x*d (O)	Γ$^!$ XI 28 (A)	
		Ω$^!$ (A)	*x*m 4d (A)	Γ$^!$ (O)	
[14]	17	Σ$^!$ VII 10 (C)	1m 16d (C)	Ξ$^!$ VIII 26 (CG)	8m 20d (C)
		VII 10 (G)			8m 21d (G)
	50	Ω VII 11 (A)	1m 17d (A)	Γ VIII 28 (A)	
	60	Ω 11 (N)			
		Ω 3 (R)	1m 7d (R)	VIII 28 (R)	
		VII (B)		VIII 27 (B)	
[15]	18	Σ V 20 (C)	2m 15d (C)	Ξ VIII 5 (C)	9$^!$ m 0d (C)
		Σ V 21 (G)		Ξ IX 5 (G)	11$^!$ m 0d (G)
	47	Σ (Q)	1 + *x*d (O)	Ξ (A)	

[6]This is assumed to be the attested VI$_2$ in Ammiṣaduqa 11.

[7]Including the attested XII$_2$ in Ammiṣaduqa 13; if the alleged VI$_2$ in Ammiṣaduqa 14 is correct, the interval is 9$^!$ m 29d.

(Table IV continued)

Year	Omens	Last visibility	Interval of invisibility	First visibility	Interval of visibility
[16]	19	Ω V 5 (C)	15d (C)	Γ IV 20 (G)	7$^!$ m 25d (G)
		Ω VIII 5 (G)		Ξ$^!$ V 20 (C)	6$^!$ m 25d (C)
	45	Ω (Q)			
[16]	20	Σ XII 15 (CG)	3m 9d (C)	Ξ III 25 (C)	8m 15d (C)
		Σ (H)	2m 7d (H)	Ξ (G)	
	58	Σ (AUV)	2m 7d (AJ)	Ξ (A)	
				III 4 (J)	
[17]	21	XII 10 (C)	4d (CH)	Γ XII 14 (C)	
	59	Ω (A)	4d (AJ)	Γ XII 14 (J)	
		Σ$^!$ (V)		Γ (A)	
[19]	34	Ω VI_2 1 (C)	15d (C)	Γ VI_2[8] 17 (C)	9$^!$ m 8d (C)
		Ω (N)	16d (M)	VI_2 (M)	
				VI_2 14 (N)	9$^!$ m 11d (N)
[20]	35	Σ III 25 (C)	2m 6d (C)	Ξ VI 24 (C)	8[9]m 3d (C)
		25 (N)	2m 16d (M)	VI 14 or *x* (N)	
				Ξ (M)	
	42	III (V)	1$^?$ m 9d (V)	Ξ (V)	
				x + 5 (K)	
[21]	36	Ω I 27 (C)	7d (C)	II 3 (C)	8m 25d (C + O)
		27 or 28 (N)			
	39	I 26 (PT)	6d (T)	Γ II 3 (P)	
		Σ$^!$ I 27 (K)		Γ (T)	
				Ξ$^!$ II 3 (K)	
[21]	37	Σ (C)		XII 28 (C)	
	56	Σ 28 (O)	2m 0d (A)	Ξ (OU)	
		Σ (A)	*x*m 0d (J)		

[8] This is assumed to be the attested VI_2 in Ammiṣaduqa 17 + d.

[9] Including a VI_2 or a XII_2; this is assumed to be the attested XII_2 in Ammiṣaduqa 17 + a.

Suggestions for a History of the Tradition of the Text.

From the preceding table two things are clear: the source of section IV, which we will henceforth call the γ text, was a rearrangement of the omens that appear in sections I and III, which sections we will call the β text; and γ does not copy all of these omens but omits omens 10 and 11 of section I and omen 34 of section III. If we look more closely, we notice that omen 34 uniquely begins with an intercalary month; that omen 10 is not an omen but as presently preserved is in the form of a simple observation dated in the year of the Golden Throne, which is the eighth year of the reign of Ammiṣaduqa; and that omen 11 contains an egregious error. For in omen 11 the western last visibility (or first invisibility) should be dated XII 11 instead of III 11 and the interval of invisibility should be 4 days instead of 9 months and 4 days. The correct data are found in omen 21, which is quoted in the γ text as omen 59. One may hypothesize therefrom that the common source of β and γ , which source we will call a, had omen 21 in place of omen 11, but that β substituted for it omen 11 with the apodosis of omen 37. Omen 21 was then added at the end of the second 8-year period and has a double apodosis, one unique to it, the other the apodosis of omens 11 and 37. Of course it is also possible to regard omen 21 as containing the first pair of phenomena in the third 8-year cycle of Venus in Ammiṣaduqa's reign.

But it seems to us that the a text naturally falls into three sections. Omens 1-10 constitute an 8-year cycle of Venus (five synodic periods) in which omen 10 was already incomplete, but was dated. Except for the wrong month in omen 4 (month VII written by mistake for month IV, an easy error to make paleographically and one that was peculiar to β since γ, in omen 43, must have had month IV), for variant day-numbers in the different sources of omen 6, and for a serious problem in omen 9, this section in β makes perfect sense astronomically as a sequence of observed events if month XII_2 was intercalated in year 4 and month VI_2 in year 5. In fact, we know that the first of these intercalations and probably the second occurred during the reign of Ammiṣaduqa. The γ text provides us with variant day-numbers for omens 1, 5, and 7 which attest to some insecurity in the text of these ten omens, but not much. This part of the text allows one to eliminate most years in the approximate time of Ammiṣaduqa from consideration as the first year of his reign, but they do not definitely decide which of the remaining years is the correct one.

Omens 11-20/21 appear to represent a second 8-year period of Venus (or such an 8-year period followed by the first pair of phenomena in a third). However, the text of β is extremely corrupt: omens 11, 14, 16, 17, 19, and 20, are impossible; van der Waerden's method of dealing with this is displayed in Table V. In fact, of the twenty-two entries in omens 11-21, which he takes to be a continuation of omens 1-10, van der Waerden, applying the 8-year rule, rejects or alters nine, reads unattested numbers in two, and rejects two entries among the nineteen of omens 1-10 because they do not fit in with the entries for eight years later in omens 11-21. Therefore, more than half of the entries in this section of β are, according to van der Waerden, astronomically impossible if omens 11-21 are to be regarded as a continuation of omens 1-10. Moreover, the versions of omens 12-21 in the γ text offer variants for eight of the day-numbers; and in nine cases no numbers happen to be preserved.

That some of these corruptions already existed in the a text is clear from the fact that the impossible interval between Σ and Ξ in omen 14–5 months and 16 days–also appears in omen 39 of the γ text as 5 months and 17 or 18 days. However, in the case of omen 16 (β), which is not correct according to van der Waerden, there is a given interval of 15 days which does not fit the dates of the phenomena; in the corresponding omen 55 (γ), the phenomena, the dates, and the interval are all different, the interval being 1 month and 4 days. The succeeding omen 17 (β) has the wrong phenomena, while omen 50 (γ) has the correct phenomena. All three texts–a, β, and γ–are corrupt in this section. Omen 20 (β) and omen 58 (γ) allow one to restore the text of this omen in a; the date of the eastern last visibility was XII 25, the interval was 2 months and 9 days, and the date of the western first visibility was III 4. The dates in omen 19 (one must either read the second date as IV 20 as does G or assume an intercalated VI_2, which is not attested for the 16th year of Ammiṣaduqa) were also copied differently from a by different scribes.

Table V. The Data as Accepted by van der Waerden.

Omen	Last visibility	First visibility
1	Ω XI 15	Γ XI 18
2	Σ VIII 11	Ξ X 19
3	Ω VI 23	Γ VII 13
4	Σ IV[1] 2	Ξ VI 3
5	Ω II 2	Γ ——
6	Σ IX 25[2]	Ξ XI 29[2]
7	Ω VIII 28	Γ IX 1
8	Σ V 21	Ξ VIII 2
9	Ω ——	Γ V 2
10	Σ XII 25	
11	Ω XII[3] 11	Γ XII 15
12	Σ VIII 10	Ξ X 16
13	Ω VI 26	Γ VI_2 8
14	Σ ——	Ξ ——
15	Ω ——	Γ II 12
16	Σ X 21	Ξ XII 21[4]
17	Ω[5] ——	Γ[5] VIII 28
18	Σ V 20	Ξ VIII[6] 5
19	Ω IV[7] 5	Γ IV[8] 20
20	Σ XII 25[9]	Ξ ——
21	Ω XII 11	Γ ——
34	Ω ——	Γ ——
35	Σ III 25	Ξ ——
36	Ω I 27	Γ II 3
37	Σ X 28	Ξ XII 28

[1]Corrected from VII in B; presumably IV in V.

[2]IX 12 in AO; XI 16 in A.

[3]Corrected from III in AC.

[4]XI 11 in CG, XI 28 in A.

[5]Σ in C; Ξ in CG.

[6]VIII in C, IX in G.

[7]V in C, VIII in G.

[8]IV in G, V in C.

[9]XII 15 in CG.

These considerations make it difficult to place much reliance on the data in this set of omens, and even raise the possibility that they are not a continuation of omens 1-10 intended to cover the 9th through the 16th (17th if omen 21 is regarded as the beginning of a third 8-year cycle) years of Ammiṣaduqa's reign. It is true that the periods of visibility indicate the presence of an intercalated VI_2 in year 11; in fact, our list of intercalations in Ammiṣaduqa's reign in Table VI shows 10**, 11**, and 13* ; and perhaps 14**. However, the text of the dates of the phenomena in years 13 and 14 (omens 16 and 17) is corrupt, so that some doubt is thrown upon 13*. Therefore, the possibility exists that omens 18-20–and perhaps omens 14-20–have nothing to do with the reign of Ammiṣaduqa, or some of them may while others do not. However one looks at the matter, it is extremely risky to use any of this section as a criterion for dating; essentially one is forced to assume, if one does use it, that disagreements of the text with computations for one's chosen date are scribal errors, so that the chosen date becomes a means of verifying the authenticity of the text rather than the other way around.

Table VI. Attested Intercalations in the Reign of Ammiṣaduqa.

(L.-F: S. Langdon and J. K. Fotheringham, *The Venus Tablets of Ammizaduga,* Oxford-London 1928, p. 61.

YOS 13: J. J. Finkelstein, *Late Old Babylonian Documents and Letters,* Yale Oriental Series 13, New Haven-London 1972.[1]

VAS 18: H. Klengel, *Altbabylonische Rechts- und Wirtschaftsurkunden,* Vorderasiatische Schriftdenkmäler Neue Folge, Heft II (Heft XVIII), Berlin 1973.)

4* (with XII_2)	L-F
5** (with VI_2)	L-F[2]
10**	L-F; YOS 13 532
11**	L-F
13*	YOS 13 404
14**	L-F[3]
17+a*	L-F; YOS 13 53; VAS 18 99
17+d**	YOS 13 146

Further, L-F cite an unpublished text dated 17+a that indicates that the preceding year contained an intercalated VI_2.

---

[1]Intercalations attested in YOS 13 have been collected and kindly communicated to us by Dr. Hermann Hunger, University of Vienna.

[2]This VI_2 is based on two unpublished contracts communicated to Fotheringham by Schnabel. It has not been confirmed.

[3]This is reported to be in an unpublished contract communicated to Fotheringham by Schnabel. If it is genuine, the interval of visibility between omens 16 and 17 is too long. Dr. Horst Klengel, Deutsche Akademie der Wissenschaften, Berlin, to whom we are grateful for his help, informs us that a quick check of the unpublished Old Babylonian contracts in the Berlin museum failed to turn up the contracts which supposedly contain the otherwise unattested intercalations.

Following omen 21 is an insert with a completely schematic arrangement of the first and last visibilities of Venus. The author of this insert assumed the following mean values for the periods of visibility and invisibility:

	Visibility	Invisibility
East	8 months 5 days	3 months
West	8 months 5 days	7 days

The preserved copies of the text contain some errors, but they are easily corrected. The subscript in MSS. C, M (= A?), and N indicates that they were copied from an original from Babylon. Note that *Iqqur īpuš* excerpts omens *only* from this section of Tablet 63. This schematic representation must be relatively late as it is based on a recognition of the periodicity of Venus' motion.

To us it seems likely that whoever put together α used four sources: one contained omens 1-10 and some of omens 11-21, another the rest of omens 11-21, a third the insert (which we will call δ), and a fourth omens 34-37. This reconstruction would support our theory that omens 34-37 have nothing to do with Ammiṣaduqa's reign.

It is also possible that the compiler of α copied from one text containing omens 1-37 till he had finished omen 21; then turned to another source, the δ text; and finally turned back to his original source to copy omens 34-37, in the process omitting the entry for Ammiṣaduqa's 18th year. This is the reconstruction of events that previous scholars have accepted; to us it appears very dubious indeed. For in fact omens 34-37 fit very poorly indeed with the previous omens. There are serious astronomical problems with three of the four—34, 35, and 36; the γ text does not contain an omen corresponding to omen 34, but it has variants for two of the five attested day-numbers in 35, 36, and 37. The text preserves a VI_2 in omen 34, which is supposed to fall in the 19th year of Ammiṣaduqa; and the interval of visibility between omens 35 and 36 indicates the presence of a VI_2 or a XII_2 if these two omens are sequential; this is supposed to correspond to the 20th year of Ammiṣaduqa. We do have in our list of intercalations two years—17+d** and 17+a*—which could well be identified with years 19 and 20 of Ammiṣaduqa, though it cannot be proved that the pair of years X** and 17+a* are not years 17 and 18, or 18 and 19, or 20 and 21, or that there was not yet another intercalated VI_2 in the period between the years 16 and 20 of Ammiṣaduqa which 17+a might follow. If we read month V in omen 19, we expect a VI_2 in year 16. The principal objection to identifying 17+d** with the 19th year of Ammiṣaduqa, however, is that the dates given in omen 34 are astronomically impossible because of the 8-year rule.

Following omen 37 in the "canonical" copies of Tablet 63 (i.e., MSS. A, J, and K, and perhaps L (+) P (+) Q) is the γ text, of which we also find fragments in a number of other copies (i.e., MSS O, T (+) U, and V); T (+) U at least contained *only* γ.

Three copies (MSS. B, N, and R) evidently omitted the γ text, but add an extra omen (60). This is a version of omen 17 with the erroneous eastern last visibility of β corrected to a western last visibility. This correction also appears in omen 50 of γ, but the source of B, N, and R seems not to have known γ. That source, according to the scribe of B, dated from the reign of Sargon II (721-705 B.C.).

There is one other fragment, MS. E, which contains omens similar to those in the γ text (not β because of the sequence of two last visibilities in the East), but not identifiable with any of them. It attests to the existence of collections of similar Venus-omens different from those found in Tablet 63, and increases the probability that at least some of those from among omens 11-21 and 34-37 preserve records of observations not made during the reign of Ammiṣaduqa.

In conclusion we would remark that this text has undergone a considerable process of expansion and corruption prior to its being inscribed on the tablets available to us. The dates of original observations of first and last visibilities of the planet–including a whole series of such from the first half or more of Ammiṣaduqa's reign–were arranged in pairs, though not always correctly. At some time each pair was associated with an apodosis; and either then or at some other time the intervals of invisibility were computed. Several such collections–or perhaps just one that was already extremely corrupt–were combined to form α; and a rearrangement of the material in α was made to form γ. We have independent witnesses to the existence of α by itself (MSS. B, N, and R, which add the extra omen 60 which is a corrected version of 17); to γ by itself (MS. T(+)U and perhaps others); and to δ by itself (K.3170 + in Appendix A together with *Iqqur īpuš*). We can only conjecture about the relationship of these separate texts to each other, and about the relationship of the dates preserved in various of them to the occurrences of phenomena during the reign of Ammiṣaduqa. That the majority of the dates of the first 8-year cycle and of the beginning of the second form a valid negative argument for establishing the date of the beginning of Ammiṣaduqa's reign seems to us to be admissible. We do not see the absolute necessity of accepting the hypothesis that the dates preserved in the rest of the text must also belong to Ammiṣaduqa's reign; at least half of them anyway are rejected or emended by those who claim they are relevant to the problem of Ammiṣaduqa's chronology. To leave out of consideration omens 11-37 will not affect the usefulness of the test of proposed dates afforded by omens 1-10 since the later dates are in any case ignored when they disagree astronomically with the earlier.

Bibliography

The following annotated bibliography includes the more significant studies of the Venus Tablets since the edition of Langdon, Fotheringham, and Schoch in 1928; they discuss the literature before 1928 in chapter V (pp. 28-44).

1. S. Langdon, J. K. Fotheringham, and C. Schoch, *The Venus Tablets of Ammizaduga,* Oxford-London 1928.

   Analysing the material on the basis of Langdon's copies, transliterations, and translations of A, B, C, G, P, Q, and part of T (Rm. 134) and using Schoch's tables, Fotheringham chose out of the possibilities -1976, -1920, -1856, -1808, and -1800 the second (-1920) to be the first year of Ammiṣaduqa's reign. Langdon misread some numbers, but essentially the table on p. 58 correctly represents the data in the copies accessible to him; the main corrections one would have to make are in omens 16, 19, and 21.

2. D. Sidersky, "Nouvelle étude sur la chronologie de la dynastie Ḫammurapienne," *Revue d'assyriologie* 37 (1940) 45-54.

   Using Langdon's data, Sidersky chose -1701 as the first year of Ammiṣaduqa.

3. A. Ungnad, *Die Venustafeln und das neunte Jahr Samsuilunas (1741 v. Chr.),* Leipzig 1940, reprinted Osnabrück 1972.

   Using A, B, C, G, P, and part of T (Rm. 134), correcting Langdon's readings at several points, and assuming that the first year of Ammiṣaduqa's reign falls between -1659 and -1639, Ungnad chose -1645 as the most probable.

4. J. W. S. Sewell in S. Smith, *Alalakh and Chronology,* London 1940, pp. 26-27 and 50-52.

   Using Langdon's data and Schoch's tables, Sewell shows that the year -1645 could be the first year of Ammiṣaduqa as well as -1920.

5. F. Cornelius, "Berossos und die altorientalische Chronologie," *Klio* 35 (1942) 1-16.

   Using Langdon's data and Schoch's and P. V. Neugebauer's tables, Cornelius claims in fn. 2 on p. 7 to have found that -1581 is a possible first year of Ammiṣaduqa.

6. B. L. van der Waerden, "On Babylonian Astronomy I. The Venus Tablets of Ammiṣaduqa," *Ex oriente lux* 10 (1945-1948) 414-424.

   "Correcting" the data of Langdon and Ungnad (see Table V), and preparing new astronomical tables to replace Schoch's (B.L. van der Waerden, "Die Berechnung der Ersten und Letzten Sichtbarkeit von Mond und Planeten und die Venustafeln des Ammisaduqa," *BSAW,* Math.-Phys. Kl. 94 [1943] 23-56), van der Waerden examines Sidersky's, Ungnad's, and Cornelius' dates, and finds the last to be the best. Therefore, he identifies -1581 with the first year of Ammiṣaduqa, but calls attention to a difficulty that this dating raises involving climatic changes in antiquity. This dating is iterated by van der Waerden in his *Die Anfange der Astronomie,* Groningen 1965, pp. 34-47.

7. J. D. Weir, *The Venus Tablets of Ammizaduga,* Istanbul 1972.

Using Langdon's data, Weir concludes that the first year of Ammiṣaduqa was -1645. Further, by making totally unjustifiable assumptions about the nature of the material preserved in the tablets, he tries to squeeze from these very questionable data arguments to support his theses that the original observations were made at Agade and that the orbit of Venus has altered since the seventeenth century B.C.

On the uncertainty of all such attempts at dating these tablets absolutely see O. Neugebauer, "Zur Frage der astronomischen Fixierung der babylonischen Chronologie," *OLZ* 32 (1929) 913-921.

THE TEXT

Introductory Note.

The format of the text edition is an experiment designed to present each text separately[1] so that the preserved parts of each manuscript may be easily identified, and at the same time each omen may be given in its most complete form.

The top line is a composite transliteration from all available manuscripts; the bottom line gives a connected transcription of this composite text. Restorations appear in these two lines only. Under the top line, each source manuscript is given a separate line; each sign that is preserved in the source is indicated by a dash under the transliterated sign in the top line. A ϕ under the transliterated sign indicates that the sign is missing in the manuscript. Broken parts are left blank within the brackets. A small raised number before a sign indicates the line division within that manuscript. Whenever variant spellings appear in the different sources, the particular spelling of that word is given for each source, e.g., the spellings *uḫ-ḫa-ram-ma* or ZAL-ma in omen 34.

Whenever the dates—month or days—of the Venus phenomena differ from text to text, the reconstructed top and bottom lines express no choice among them. When the month name differs, these lines have MN, and the different months are given in each source line; when the day-number differs, these lines have UD.n.KAM, and the attested day-numbers are given in each source line.

Translations accompany the first two omens only, since the protases of omens 1-21 and 34-60 are of the same pattern (see p. 9f). The variables in the protases—the dates of first invisibility, duration of invisibility, and first visibility, and the Eastern or Western occurrence of these phenomena—are given for the sake of clarity and easy comparison in Table IV. Translation and comments on the protases of omens 22-33 are given on p. 10. The translation of the apodoses is found in Table II.

[1]For this format, sometimes referred to as a "score", see D. O. Edzard, Or. NS 43 (1974) 106.

Transliteration and Transcription

1	DIŠ	[ina]	ITI.ÁŠ	UD.15.KAM	^{d}Nin-si$_{4}$-an-na	ina	^{d}UTU.ŠÚ.A	it-bal	UD.3.KAM
A ^{1}[					] -	-	- - - - - -	- -	- - -
B ^{1} ⌈-⌉		[ ]	- -	- - -	- - - - - -	-	- - - - - -	- -	- - -
¶		*[Ina]*	*Šabāṭi*	UD.15.KAM	*Ninsianna*	*ina*	*ereb šamši*	*itbal*	*3 ūmī*
		In month XI,		15th day,	Venus	in the west		disappeared,	3 days

	ina	AN-e	uḫ-ḫa-ram-ma	ina	ITI.ÁŠ	UD.18.KAM	^{d}Nin-si$_{4}$-an-na
A	-	- -	- - - - -	^{2} [			]- - -
B	-	[	]	^{2} -	- -	- - -	- - - - - -
	ina	*šamê*	*uḫḫaramma*	*ina*	*Šabāṭi*	UD.18.KAM	*Ninsianna*
	in the sky		it stayed away, and	in month XI,		18th day,	Venus

	ina	^{d}UTU.È	IGI.DU$_{8}$	IDIM.MEŠ	DU$_{8}$.MEŠ	^{d}IM	ŠÈG.MEŠ-šú	^{d}É-a
A	-	- - -	- -	- -	- -	^{3}[		]
B	-	- - -	- -	- -	[ ]	^{3}- -	- - - -	- - -
	ina	*ṣīt šamši*	*innamir:*	*nagbū*	*ippaṭṭaru*	*Adad*	*zunnēšu*	*Ea*
	in the east		became visible:	springs	will open,	Adad	his rain,	Ea

	IDIM.MEŠ-šú	ub-ba-la	LUGAL	ana	LUGAL	SILIM.MA	KIN
A	- - - -	- - -	-	-	-	- -	-
B	- - - -	- - -	-	-	-	S[ILIM	]
	nagbēšu	*ubbala*	*šarru*	*ana*	*šarri*	*salīma*	*išappar.*
	his floods	will bring,	king	to king		messages of reconciliation	will send (= apodosis 13).

2	DIŠ	ina	ITI.APIN	UD.11.KAM	^{d}Nin-si$_{4}$-an-na	ina	^{d}UTU.È	it-bal	2	ITI
A ^{4}[					] -	-	- - - -	- -		- -
B ^{4} -		-	- - -	- - -	- - - - - -	-	- - - -	- -		- -
¶		*Ina*	*Araḫsamna*	UD.11.KAM	*Ninsianna*	*ina*	*ṣīt šamši*	*itbal*	*2*	*arḫī*
		In month VIII,		11th day,	Venus	in the east		disappeared;	2	months

	UD.n.KAM	ina	AN-e	uḫ-ḫa-ram-ma	*ina*	ITI.AB	UD.n.KAM
A	- 8 -	-	- -	- - - -	^{5} [		
B	- 7 -	-	- -	- [ ]	^{5} -	- -	- 19 -
	n ūmī	*ina*	*šamê*	*uḫḫaramma*	*ina*	*Ṭebēti*	UD.n. KAM
	n days	in the sky		it stayed away, and	in month X,		nth day,

	^{d}Nin-si$_{4}$-an-na	ina	^{d}UTU.ŠÚ.A	IGI.DU$_{8}$	EBUR	KUR	SI.SÁ
A	n]a	-	- - - - -	- -	-	-	- -
B	- - - - - -	-	- - - - - -	- -	-	-	- [ ]
	Ninsianna	*ina*	*ereb šamši*	*innamir:*	*ebūr*	*māti*	*iššir.*
	Venus	in the west		became visible: the harvest of the land will prosper (= apodosis 1).			

[*BM* 2, 29]

3 DIŠ ina ITI.KIN UD.23.KAM ^{d}Nin-si$_{4}$-an-na ina ^{d}UTU.ŠÚ.A it-bal UD.20.KAM ina AN-e
A ^{6}[n]a - - - - - - - - - - - - -
B ^{6} -
¶ *Ina Ulūli* UD.23.KAM *Ninsianna ina ereb šamši itbal 20 ūmī ina šamê*

uḫ-ḫa-ram-ma ina ITI.DU$_{6}$ UD.13.KAM ^{d}Nin-si$_{4}$-an-na ina ^{d}UTU.È IGI.DU$_{8}$
A - - - - ^{7}[n]a - - - - - - -
B - - - [ ] ^{7}- - - - - - - - - - - - - - - - - -
uḫḫaramma ina Tašrīti UD.13.KAM *Ninsianna ina ṣīt šamši innamir:*

NAM.KÚR.MEŠ ina KUR GÁL.MEŠ EBUR SI.SÁ
A NAM - - - - - - - - -
B SAL - - - - - - - [ ]
J^{6}* [ ] - [ ]
nukurātu ina māti ibaššâ ebūru iššir.

---

4 DIŠ ina ITI.DU$_{6}$ UD.2.KAM ^{d}Nin-si$_{4}$-an-na ina ^{d}UTU.È it-bal 2 ITI UD.1.KAM ina
A ^{8}[ ] - - - - - - - - - - - - -
B ^{8} -
J ^{7}[
¶ *Ina Tašrīti* UD.2.KAM *Ninsianna ina ṣīt šamši itbal 2 arḫī* UD.1.KAM *ina*

AN-e uḫ-ḫa-ram-ma ina ITI.KIN UD.3.KAM ^{d}Nin-si$_{4}$-an-na ina ^{d}UTU.ŠÚ.A IGI.DU$_{8}$
A - - - - - - - ^{9}[ ] - - - - - - -
B - - - - [ ]^{9} -
J IT]I - - - - [^{8}]
šamê uḫḫaramma ina Ulūli UD.3.KAM *Ninsianna ina ereb šamši innamir:*

ŠÀ KUR DÙG-ab
A - - - -
B - - - [ ]
J - - [ ]
libbi māti iṭâb.

* J 1-5 broken.

5	DIŠ	ina	ITI.GUD	UD.2.KAM	^{d}Nin-si$_4$-an-na	ina	^{d}UTU.ŠÚ.A	it-bal	UD.n.KAM	ina	AN-e
A 10	[					]	⌜-⌝ - - -	- -	- 15 -	-	- -
B 10	-	-	- -	- - -	- - - - - -	-	- - - -	- -	- 18 -	-	- -
J 9	[										]
¶	*Ina*	*Ajari*	UD.2.KAM	*Ninsianna*	*ina*	*ereb šamši*	*itbal*	*n ūmī*	*ina*	*šamê*	

	uḫ-ḫa-ram-ma	ina	ITI.GUD	UD.n.KAM	^{d}Nin-si$_4$-an-na	ina	^{d}UTU.È	IGI.DU$_8$	ŠÈG.ME
A	uḫ-ḫa-ram-ma 11	[	] -	[			] - -	- - -	- -
B	uḫ-ḫa-ram-ma 11	-	- -	- 18 -	- - - - - -	-	- - -	- - - -	- -
J	ZAL	-	- -	- [10					
	uḫḫaramma	*ina*	*Ajari*	UD.n.KAM	*Ninsianna*	*ina*	*ṣīt šamši*	*innamir:*	*zunnū*

	u	A.KAL.ME	GÁL.ME	EBUR	KUR	SI.SÁ
A	-	- - -	- ME	-	-	- -
B	-	- - -	- MEŠ	-	-	- -
J			M]EŠ	-	-	- -
	u	*mīlū*	*ibaššû*	*ebūr*	*māti*	*iššir.*

6	DIŠ	ina	ITI.GAN	UD.n.KAM	^{d}Nin-si$_4$-an-na	ina	^{d}UTU.È	it-bal	2	ITI	UD.4.KAM	ina
A 12	-	-	- -	- ⌜12⌝ [			] -	- -	-	-	- - -	-
B 12	-	-	- -	- 25 -	- - - - - -	-	- - - -	- -	-	-	- - -	-
J 11	[										]- -	-
¶	*Ina*	*Kislimi*	UD.n.KAM	*Ninsianna*	*ina*	*ṣīt šamši*	*itbal*	*2*	*arḫī*	*4 ūmī*	*ina*	

	AN-e	uḫ-ḫa-ram-ma	ina	ITI.ÁŠ	UD.n.KAM	^{d}Nin-si$_4$-an-na	ina	^{d}UTU.ŠÚ.A	IGI.DU$_8$
A	- -	uḫ-ḫa-ram-ma 13	-	- -	- 16 -	- - - - - -	[	] - -	- -
B	- -	uḫ-ḫa-ram-ma 13	-	- -	- 29 -	- - - - - -	-	- - - -	- - -
J	- -	[ZAL - m]a	-	- -	- 28 -	12[			]
	šamê	*uḫḫaramma*	*ina*	*Šabāṭi*	UD.n.KAM	*Ninsianna*	*ina*	*ereb šamši*	*innamir:*

	EBUR	KUR	SI.SÁ
A	-	-	- -
B	-	-	- -
J	-	-	- [ ]
	ebūr	*māti*	*iššir.*

7 DIŠ ina ITI.APIN UD.n.KAM ^{d}Nin-si$_{4}$-an-na ina ^{d}UTU.ŠÚ.A it-bal UD.3.KAM ina
A [14] - - - - - 20 $^{hi-pí\ eš-šú}$ - - - - - - - [i]t - - - - -
B [14] - - - - - 18.KAM - - - - - - - - - - - - - - - - - -
J [13] [ ]
¶ *Ina Araḫsamna* UD.n.KAM *Ninsianna ina ereb šamši itbal 3 ūmī ina*

AN-e uḫ-ḫa-ram-ma ina ITI.GAN UD.1.KAM ^{d}Nin-si$_{4}$-an-na ina ^{d}UTU.È IGI.DU$_{8}$
A - - uḫ-ḫa-ram-ma [15] - - - - - - - - - - - - - [
B - - uḫ-ḫa-ram-ma [15] - - - - - - - - - - - - - - - - - -
D [1'] [
J - - ZAL [ ] - - - - [[14]
šamê uḫḫaramma ina Kislimi UD.1.KAM *Ninsianna ina ṣīt šamši innamir:*

SU.KÚ ŠE u IN.NU ina KUR GÁL ub-bu-tu GAR.ME
A S]U - - - - - - - - - - : - - - - - -
B - - - - - - - - - - KI.MIN - - - - - -
D]ŠU - - - ⌜ (traces) ⌝
J]- - - ϕ - - t[u]
ḫušaḫḫi še'i u tibni ina māti ibašši ubbutu iššakkan.

---

8 DIŠ ina ITI.NE UD.21.KAM ^{d}Nin-si$_{4}$-an-na ina ^{d}UTU.È it-bal 2 ITI UD.11.KAM ina
A [16] - - - - - - - - - - - - - - - - - - [1⌉1⌜ - ⌝ -
B [16] [ ] - - - - - - - - - 11 - -
C [1'] [ ]⌜- - ⌝ - [ ] [2'] [
D [2'] [b]al ϕ ϕ - 11 - -
J [15] [
¶ *Ina Abi* UD.21.KAM *Ninsianna ina ṣīt šamši itbal 2 arḫī 11 ūmī ina*

AN-e uḫ-ḫa-ram-ma ina ITI.APIN UD.2.KAM ^{d}Nin-si$_{4}$-an-na ina ^{d}UTU.ŠÚ.A
A - - uḫ-ḫa-ram-ma [17] - - - - - - - - - - - - - - - - -
B - - uḫ-ḫa-ram-ma [17] [ ]
C]ram-ma - - - - - - - - - - - n[a] [3'] [
D - - uḫ-ḫa-ram[ ] [3'] [ ]
J] ZAL ma - - ⌜ - ⌝ [[16]
šamê uḫḫaramma ina Araḫsamna UD.2.KAM *Ninsianna ina ereb šamši*

IGI.DU$_{8}$ ŠÈG.MEŠ ina KUR GÁL.MEŠ ub-bu-tu GAR.MEŠ
A - [G]ÁL - - - - - MEŠ
B - - - - - - - - - - - - MEŠ
C] - - - - - - - - - - - ME
D - - - ME - - - - - - - - an
J] - - - - MEŠ
innamir: zunnū ina māti ibaššû ubbutu iššakkan.

9	DIŠ	ina	ITI.ŠU	UD.25.KAM	^{d}Nin-si$_4$-an-na	ina	^{d}UTU.ŠÚ.A	it-bal	UD.7.KAM	ina	AN-e
A	18 -	-	- -	- - -	- - - - - -	-	- - - - -	- ba[l			] -
B	18 [							]	- - -	-	- -
C	4' -	-	- -	- - -	- - - - - -	-	- - - - -	- -	5' - - -	-	- -
D	4' [						]-	- -	- - -	-	- -
J	17 [									] -	- -
¶	*Ina*	*Du'ūzi*	UD.25.KAM	*Ninsianna*	*ina*	*ereb šamši*	*itbal*	*7 ūmī*	*ina*	*šamê*	

	uḫ-ḫa-ram-ma	ina	ITI.NE	UD.2.KAM	^{d}Nin-si$_4$-an-na	ina	^{d}UTU.È	IGI.DU$_8$	ŠÈG.MEŠ
A	uḫ-ḫa-ram-ma 19 -	- -	- - -	- - - - - -	-	- - - - -	D[U$_8$		
B	uḫ-ḫa-ram-ma 19 [								
C	uḫ-ḫa-ram-ma -	- -	- - -	- - - - - - 6'	-	- - - -	-	- -	
D	uḫ-ḫa-ram-ma 5' [					] -	- -	KI.MIN	
J	ZAL -	-	- -	- - - 18 [					
	uḫḫaramma	*ina*	*Abi*	UD.2.KAM	*Ninsianna*	*ina*	*ṣīt šamši*	*innamir:*	*zunnū*

	ina	KUR	GÁL.MEŠ	ub-bu-tu	GAR.MEŠ
A			] - ME	- - - -	- -
B		] -	- MEŠ	- - - -	- -
C	-	-	- MEŠ	- - - -	- -
D					
J			]	- - - -	- -
	ina	*māti*	*ibaššû*	*ubbutu*	*iššakkan.*

10	DIŠ	ina	ITI.ŠE	UD.25.KAM	^{d}Nin-si$_4$-an-na	ina	^{d}UTU.È	it-bal	MU	GIŠ.DÚR.GAR
A	20 [	]	- -	- - -	- - - - - -	[	] - -	- -	21 [	G]IŠ - -
B	20 [							] - -	21 [	
C	7' -	-	- -	- - -	- - - - - -	-	- - - -	- - 8'	-	- - -
D	6' [						]-	- -	-	- - -
J	19 [							]	-	- - -
¶	*Ina*	*Addari*	UD.25.KAM	*Ninsianna*	*ina*	*ṣīt šamši*	*itbal*	MU	GIŠ.DÚR.GAR

	KÙ.GI.GA.KAM
A	[K]Ù- - -
B	G]A -
C	- - - -
D	- - - -
J	- - - KE$_4$
	KÙ.GI.GA.KAM

11	DIŠ	ina	ITI.SIG$_4$	UD.11.KAM	^{d}Nin-si$_4$-an-na	ina	^{d}UTU.ŠÚ.A	it-bal	9	ITI	UD.n.KAM
A [22]	[		I]TI -	- - -	- - - - -	-	- - - -	- -	-	IT[I	]
B [22]	[										
C [9']	-	-	- S[IG$_4$]	- - -	- - - - -	-	- - - -	- -	-	-	- 4 -
D [7']	[						] - -	-	-		- 4 -
J [20]	[										]5 -
¶	*Ina*	*Simāni*	UD.11.KAM	*Ninsianna*	*ina*	*ereb šamši*	*itbal*	*9*	*arhī*	*n ūmī*	

	ina	AN-e	uh-ha-ram-ma	ina	ITI.ŠE	UD.n.KAM	^{d}Nin-si$_4$-an-na	ina	^{d}UTU.È
A	-	- -	uh-ha-ram-ma [23] [		I]TI -	- 15 -	- - - - - -	-	- - -
B		]⌈-⌉	uh-ha-ram-ma [23] [						
C	-	- -	uh-ha-ram-ma [10'] -	-	- -	- 15 -	φ φ φ φ φ	-	- - -
D	-	- - [8'] [						]	- - -
J	-	- -	ZAL	-	- - -	- 16 -	[21] [		
	ina	*šamê*	*uhharamma*	*ina*	*Addari*	UD.n.KAM	*Ninsianna*	*ina*	*ṣīt šamši*

	IGI.DU$_8$	LUGAL	ana	LUGAL	LÚ.NE	KIN-ár
A	- -	[		]	LÚ.NE	- -
B						]-
C	- -	-	-	-	SILIM.MA	- -
D	- -	-	-	-	LÚ.NE	- -
J	] -	-	-	-	LÚ.NE	- -
	innamir:	*šarru*	*ana*	*šarri*	*ṣalta*	*išappar.* (var.: *salīma išappar*)

12	DIŠ	ina	ITI.APIN	UD.10.KAM	^{d}Nin-si$_4$-an-na	ina	^{d}UTU.È	it-bal	2	ITI	UD.n.KAM	ina
A [24]	[		IT]I -	- - -	- - - - -	-	- - - -	- -	[		]	-
C [11']	-	-	- -	- - -	- - - - -	-	- - - -	- -	-	-	- 6 -	-
D [9']	[						]⌈-	- ⌉	[	]	⌈- 6⌉ -	-
J [22]	[											
F [1']	[						]⌈-	-	-	-	- 16? -	-
¶	*Ina*	*Arahsamna*	UD.10.KAM	*Ninsianna*	*ina*	*ṣīt šamši*	*itbal*	*2*	*arhī*	*n ūmī*	*ina*	

	AN-e	uh-ha-ram-ma	ina	ITI.AB	UD.16.KAM	ina	^{d}UTU.ŠÚ.A	IGI.DU$_8$	EBUR
A	- -	uh-ha-ram-ma [25] [		A]B	- - -	⌈-	- - ⌉[	]	-
C	- -	ZAL	- [12'] -	- -	- - -	-	- - - -	- DU$_8$	-
D	- - [10'] [							]	⌈ -
J		ZAL	m]a	-	- - -	-	- - - -	- DU$_8$	-
F	- - ⌉ [								
	šamê	*uhharamma*	*ina*	*Ṭebēti*	UD.16.KAM	*ina*	*ereb šamši*	*innamir:*	*ebūr*

	KUR	SI.SÁ
A	-	- -
C	-	- -
D	-	- -⌉
J	-	- -
F		]
	māti	*iššir.*

13	DIŠ	ina	ITI.KIN	UD.26.KAM	^{d}Nin-si$_4$-an-na	ina	^{d}UTU.ŠÚ.A	it-bal	UD.11.KAM	ina	AN-e
A	26 [										
C	13' -	-	- -	- - -	- - - - -	-	- - - -	- -	- - -	-	- -
F	2' [						] - -	- -	- - -	-	- -
J	23 [										
¶		*Ina*	*Ulūli*	UD.26.KAM	*Ninsianna*	*ina*	*ereb šamši*	*itbal*	*11 ūmī*	*ina*	*šamê*

	uḫ-ḫa-ram-ma	ina	ITI.KIN.2.KAM	UD.7.KAM	ina	^{d}UTU.È	IGI.DU$_8$	ŠÀ	KUR	DÙG-ab
A	] - - -	27 [							]	- -
C	ZA[L]	14' -	- - - -	- - - -	-	- ⌜-⌝	- -	-	-	[ ]
F	ZAL -	-	- [							]
J	]	-	- ⌜ - ⌝- -	- - - -	-	- -	- ϕ	-	-	- -
	uḫḫaramma	*ina*	*Ulūli arkî*	UD.7.KAM	*ina*	*ṣīt šamši*	*innamir:*	*libbi*	*māti*	*iṭâb.*

14	DIŠ	ina	ITI.BÁR	UD.9.KAM	^{d}Nin-si$_4$-an-na	ina	^{d}UTU.È	it-bal	5	ITI	UD.16.KAM	ina
A	28 [											
C	15' -	-	- -	- - -	- - - - -	⌜-	- - -⌝	- -	-	-	- -	-
F	3' [						]	- -	-	-	- -	-
J	24 [											
¶		*Ina*	*Nisanni*	UD.9.KAM	*Ninsianna*	*ina*	*ṣīt šamši*	*itbal*	*5*	*arḫī*	*16 ūmī*	*ina*

	AN-e	uḫ-ḫa-ram-ma	ina	ITI.KIN	UD.25.KAM	ina	^{d}UTU.ŠÚ.A	IGI.DU$_8$	ŠÀ
A		r]am -	[						
C	- [-	ZAL -]	16' -	- -	- - -	-	- - - -	- - -	-
F	- -	[							
J				K]IN	- - -	-	- - - -	- ϕ	-
	šamê	*uḫḫaramma*	*ina*	*Ulūli*	UD.25.KAM	*ina*	*ereb šamši*	*innamir:*	*libbi*

	KUR	DÙG-ab
A		]
C	-	[ ]
F		]
J	-	- -
	māti	*iṭâb.*

15 DIŠ ina ITI.GUD UD.5.KAM ^{d}Nin-si$_4$-an-na ina ^{d}UTU.ŠÚ.A it-bal UD.7.KAM ina AN-e
C 17' - 7 UD-me - - -
F 4' [ ] - - UD.7.KAM - - -
G 1' [ ] UD.7.KAM [
J 25 [
¶ *Ina Ajari* UD.5.KAM *Ninsianna ina ereb šamši itbal 7 ūmī ina šamê*

ZAL-ma ina ITI.[GUD] UD.12.KAM ina ^{d}UTU.È IGI.DU$_8$ EBUR KUR SI.SÁ
C - [ ]18'- - - - - - - - - - :
F - - - [5' 11]+1- - - - - SAR [ ]
G]2' - - [ ] - 12 - - -[ ]
J]- IGI *ϕ* - - - [ ]
uḫḫaramma ina [*Ajari*] UD.12.KAM *ina ṣīt šamši innamir: ebūr māti iššir.*

---

16 DIŠ ina ITI.AB UD.n.KAM ^{d}Nin-si$_4$-[an-na] ina ^{d}UTU.È it-bal UD.15.KAM ina AN-e
C 18' - - - A[B] - 20 - - - - [ ]19' - - - - - - - - - - - - -
G 3' - - - ⌜-⌝ - 21 - -[
J 26 [
¶ *Ina Ṭebēti* UD.n.KAM *Ninsi*[*anna*] *ina ṣīt šamši itbal 15 ūmī ina šamê*

ZAL-ma ina ITI.ÁŠ UD.11.KAM ina ^{d}UTU.ŠÚ.A [IGI.DU$_8$ . . .]
C - - - - - - - - - - - - - - - [ ]
G]4' - - - - - - - - - [ ]
J] - - - - [ ]
uḫḫaramma ina Šabāṭi UD.11.KAM *ina ereb šamši* [*innamir:*]

---

17 DIŠ ina ITI.DU$_6$ UD.10.KAM ^{d}Nin-si$_4$-an-na ina ^{d}UTU.È it-bal 1 ITI UD.16.KAM [ina
C 20' - - - ⌜-⌝ - - - - - - - - - - - - - [i]t-[b]al - - - ⌜-⌝K[AM
G 5' - - - - - - - - - - - - - [
¶ *Ina Tašrīti* UD.10.KAM *Ninsianna ina ṣīt šamši itbal 1* ITI UD.16.KAM [*ina*

AN-e ZAL-ma] ina ITI.APIN UD.26.KAM ina ^{d}UTU.ŠÚ.A IGI.DU$_8$ ŠÈG.MEŠ ina
C]21'- - - - - - - - - - - - - - - - -
G]6' - - - - - - - - - - - - - - - - [
šamê uḫḫaramma] *ina Araḫsamna* UD.26.KAM *ina ereb šamši innamir: zunnū ina*

KUR GÁL.MEŠ ub-[bu-tu GAR-an]
C - - - - [ ]
G]
māti ibaššû ub[*butu iššakkan*].

18 DIŠ ina ITI.NE UD.n.KAM ^{d}Nin-si$_4$-an-na ina ^{d}UTU.È it-bal n ITI UD.15.KAM ina
C 22' - - - - - 20 - - - - - - - - - - - - - - 2 - - - - -
G 7' - - - - - 21 - - - - - - - - - - - - [
H 1' (traces)
¶ *Ina Abi* UD.n.KAM *Ninsianna ina ṣīt šamši itbal n arḫī 15 ūmī ina*

AN-[e] uḫ-ḫa-ram-ma ina ITI.MN UD.5.KAM ^{d}Nin-si$_4$-an-na ina ^{d}UTU.ŠÚ.A
C A[N - ZAL -]23' - - ⌜APIN⌝ - - - ϕ ϕ ϕ ϕ ϕ - - - - - -
G] 8' uḫ-ḫa-ram-ma - - GAN - - - - - - - - - - - - - [
H (traces)
šamê uḫḫaramma ina ITI.MN UD.15.KAM *Ninsianna ina ereb šamši*

IGI.DU$_8$ ŠÈG.MEŠ ina KUR GÁL.MEŠ ub-bu-tu [GAR-an]
C - - - - - - - - - - b[u]
G]9' - - - [ ]
H (traces)
innamir: zunnū ina māti ibaššû ubbutu [iššakkan].

---

19 DIŠ ina ITI.MN UD.5.KAM ^{d}Nin-si$_4$-an-na ina ^{d}UTU.ŠÚ.A it-bal UD.15.KAM ina AN-e
C 24' - - - ⌜NE⌝ - [
G 10' - - - APIN - - - - - - - - - - - - - - - ⌜-⌝[
H 2' [ ]- - - - - - - - - -
¶ *Ina* ITI.MN UD.5.KAM *Ninsianna ina ereb šamši itbal 15 ūmī ina šamê*

[uḫ-ḫa-ram-ma] ina ITI.MN UD.20.KAM ina ^{d}UTU.È IGI.DU$_8$ ŠÈG.ME ina AN-e u
C ZAL -]25' - - ⌜NE⌝ - - - - - < - > - ŠÚ.A - - - - - - - ϕ
G]11' - - ŠU - - - - - - - È - - - - ϕ ϕ ϕ -
H ≪ ina A[N-e≫ 3'[
[*uḫḫaramma*] *ina* ITI.MN UD.20.KAM *ina ṣīt šamši innamir: zunnū ina šamê (u)*

A.KAL.ME ina IDIM GÁL.ME [ ]
C - - ME - - - - [ ]
G - - [ ]
H]MEŠ - - - - [ ]
mīlū ina nagbī ibaššû [ ]

20	DIŠ	ina	ITI.ŠE	UD.15.KAM	^{d}Nin-si$_{4}$-an-na	ina	^{d}UTU.È	it-bal	n	ITI	UD.n.KAM	ina
C $^{26'}$	-	-	- -	- - -	- - - - - -	-	- - - -	- -	3	-	- 9	-	-
G $^{12'}$	[		]-	- - -	- - - - - -	-	- - -	- b[al				
H $^{4'}$	[						]⌜-⌝	- -	2	-	- 7	-	-
¶		*Ina*	*Addari*	UD.15.KAM	*Ninsianna*	*ina*	*ṣīt šamši*	*itbal*	*n*	*arḫī*	*n ūmī*	*ina*

	AN-[e	uḫ-ḫa-ram-ma]	ina	ITI.MN	UD.25.KAM	ina	^{d}UTU.ŠÚ.A	IGI.DU$_{8}$	ŠUB-tim
C	[	ZAL -ma]	$^{27'}$ -	- SIG$_{4}$	- - -	-	- - - - -	- -	- -
G			$^{13'}$		] -	-	- - - - -	- -	- -
H	- [		$^{5'}$						
	šamê	[*uḫḫaramma*]	*ina*	ITI.MN	UD.25.KAM	*ina*	*ereb šamši*	*innamir:*	*miqitti*

	ERÍN	man-da	KI.MIN	ŠUB-tim	[ ]
C	-	- -	- -	- -	[ ]
G	[				]
H					]
	ummān-manda:		*miqitti*		[ ]

21	DIŠ	ina	ITI.ŠE	UD.10.KAM	^{d}Nin-si$_{4}$-an-na	[ina	^{d}UTU.ŠÚ.A]	it-bal	UD.4.KAM	ina	AN-e
C $^{28'}$	-	-	- -	- - -	- - - - - -	[	]	⌜-⌝ [ba]l	- - -	-	- -
H $^{6'}$	[							i]t -	- - -	-	- -
¶		*Ina*	*Addari*	UD.10.KAM	*Ninsianna*	[*ina*	*ereb šamši*]	*itbal*	*4 ūmī*	*ina*	*šamê*

	uḫ-ḫa-r[am-ma]	ina	ITI.ŠE	UD.14.KAM	ina	^{d}UTU.È	[IGI.DU$_{8}$]	EBUR	KI.A	SI.SÁ
C	[ZAL -ma]	$^{29'}$ -	- -	- - -	-	- - - -	[ ]	-	- -	- -
H	uḫ-ḫa-r[am-ma						$^{7'}$	LUGAL	ana	LUGAL
	uḫḫar[*amma*]	*ina*	*Addari*	UD.14.KAM	*ina*	*ṣīt šamši*	[*innamir*]	(*šarru*	*ana*	*šarri*

	ŠÀ	KUR	DÙG-ab					
C	-	-	- -					
H	SILIM.MA	KI]N-ár	E[BUR		]			
	salīma	*išappar)*	*ebūr*	*ruṭibti*	*iššir*	*libbi*	*māti*	*iṭâb.*

S$_{1}$

C $^{30'}$	(illegible traces)			
H $^{8'}$	[	]	[	]

---

22 DIŠ ina ITI.BÁR UD.2.KAM ^{d}Nin-si$_4$-an-na ina ^{d}UTU.È IGI.DU$_8$ ú-ru-ba-a-tum ina KUR
C 31' -
H 9' [ ]⌈-⌉ [ ] ⌈- - -⌉- - - -
¶ *Ina Nisanni* UD.2.KAM *Ninsianna ina ṣīt šamši innamir: urubātu ina māti*

GÁL.MEŠ EN UD.6.KAM šá ITI.GAN ina ^{d}UTU.È DU-az UD.7 šá ITI.GAN
C - - 32' -
H - - E[N 10'
ibaššâ; adi UD.6.KAM *ša Kislimi ina ṣīt šamši izzaz* UD.7 *ša Kislimi*

i-tab-bal-ma 3 ITI ina AN-e uḫ-ḫa-ram-ma UD.8.KAM šá ITI.ŠE ^{d}Nin-si$_4$-an-na
C - - - - - - - - - - - 33'- - - - - - - - - - - - - - - - - - - -
H A]N - - - - - - - - - - - - - - - - - [
itabbalma 3 arḫī ina šamê uḫḫaramma UD.8.KAM *ša Addari Ninsianna*

ina ^{d}UTU.ŠÚ.A SAR-ma LUGAL ana LUGAL SAL.KÚR KIN-ár
C - - - - - - - - - - - - - - - -
H]
ina ereb šamši inappaḫma: šarru ana šarri nukurta išappar.

---

23 DIŠ ina ITI.GUD UD.3.KAM ^{d}Nin-si$_4$-an-na ina ^{d}UTU.ŠÚ.A IGI.DU$_8$ SAL.KÚR.MEŠ ina
C 34' -
H 11' [ ]- - - - - - - - -
¶ *Ina Ajari* UD.3.KAM *Ninsianna ina ereb šamši innamir: nukurātu ina*

KUR GÁL.MEŠ EN UD.6.KAM šá ITI.AB ina ^{d}UTU.ŠÚ.A DU-az UD.7.KAM šá
C - - - 35' - - 6 - - - - - - - - - - - - - - - - - - -
H - - - - - - 7 - - - - [12'
māti ibaššâ; adi UD.6.KAM *ša Ṭebēti ina ereb šamši izzaz* UD.7.KAM *ša*

ITI.AB i-tab-bal-ma UD.7.KAM ina AN-e uḫ-ḫa-ram-ma UD.15.KAM šá ITI.AB
C - - - - - - 36' -
H m]a - - - - - - - -
Ṭebēti itabbalma 7 ūmī ina šamê uḫḫaramma UD.15.KAM *ša Ṭebēti*

^{d}Nin-si$_4$-an-na ina ^{d}UTU.È SAR-ma EBUR KUR SI.SÁ ŠÀ KUR DÙG-ab
C - - - - - 37'- - - - - - - - - - - - - - - -
H - - - - - - - - - - - S[AR]
Ninsianna ina ṣīt šamši inappaḫma: ebūr māti iššir libbi māti iṭâb.

24 DIŠ ina ITI.SIG$_4$ UD.[4].KAM* ^{d}Nin-si$_4$-an-na ina ^{d}UTU.È IGI.DU$_8$ RI.RI.GA ERÍN
C [38'] [IT]I - - [ ] - - - - - - - - - - - - - - - - -
H [13'] [ ]⌈-⌉ - - - - - -
¶ *Ina Simāni* UD.[4].KAM *Ninsianna ina ṣīt šamši innamir: miqitti ummāni*

ma-at-ti EN UD.8.KAM šá ITI.ÁŠ ina ^{d}UTU.È DU-az UD.8.KAM šá ITI.ÁŠ
C - - - [39'] ⌈- -⌉- - - - - - - - - - - - - - - - - -
H - - - - - - - - - - - [
matti; adi UD.8.KAM *ša Šabāṭi ina ṣīt šamši izzaz* UD.8.KAM *ša Šabāṭi*

i-tab-bal-ma [3] ITI ina AN-e uḫ-[ḫa]-ram-ma UD.9.KAM šá ITI.GUD
C - - - - [40'] [ ] - - - - - [- r]am - - - - - - - -
H [14']] - - - - - - - -
itabbalma [*3*] *arḫī ina šamê uḫ*[*ḫa*]*ramma* UD.9.KAM *ša Ajari*

^{d}Nin-si$_4$-an-na ina ^{d}UTU.ŠÚ.A SAR-ma SAL.KÚR.MEŠ ina KUR GÁL.MEŠ
C - - - - - [41'] - - - - - - - - - - - - - - - -
H - - - - - - - - - - [ ]
Ninsianna ina ereb šamši inappaḫma: nukurātu ina māti ibaššâ.

---

*Day 4 restored from *Iqqur īpuš*, see Appendix A.

25 [DIŠ ina ITI].ŠU UD.5.KAM ^{d}Nin-si$_{4}$-an-na ina ^{d}UTU.ŠÚ.A IGI.DU$_{8}$ SAL.KÚR.MEŠ ina
C 42' [ ] -
H 15' [ ] - - - ϕ - - - - -
L 1' [ ]⌜- - ⌝ [ ] - - - - - - ϕ - [
¶ [*Ina*] *Du'ūzi* UD.5.KAM *Ninsianna ina ereb šamši innamir: nukurātu ina*

KUR GÁL.MEŠ EBUR KUR SI.SÁ EN UD.n.KAM šá ITI.ŠE ina ^{d}UTU.ŠÚ.A
C - - - - - - - 43'- - 9 - - - - - - - - - -
H - - - - - - - 2' - - 8 - - [
L
māti ibaššâ ebūr māti iššir; adi UD.n.KAM *ša Addari ina ereb šamši*

DU-az UD.10.KAM šá ITI.ŠE TÙM -ma UD.7.KAM ina AN-e uḫ-ḫa-ram-ma
C - - - - - - - - - - - - 44'- - - - - - - - - - -
H 16'
L]⌜-⌝ - - - - - - - i-tab-bal-[ma 3'
izzaz UD.10.KAM *ša Addari itabbalma 7 ūmī ina šamê uḫḫaramma*

UD.n.KAM šá ITI.ŠE ^{d}Nin-si$_{4}$-an-na ina ^{d}UTU.È SAR-ma LUGAL ana LUGAL
C - 18 - - - - - - - - - - 45'- - - - - - - - - -
H U]D.17 - - - - - - - - - - - - - - [
L] - - - - - - - - - [
UD.n.KAM *ša Addari Ninsianna ina ṣīt šamši inappaḫma: šarru ana šarri*

SAL.KÚR KIN -ár
C - - - - -
H]
L]
nukurta išappar.

26 [DIŠ ina ITI.]NE UD.6.KAM ^{d}Nin-si$_{4}$-an-na ina ^{d}UTU.È IGI.DU$_{8}$ ŠÈG.ME ina AN-e
C r.1 [ ] -
H 17' [ ] - - - - - - -
L 4' [N]in - - - - - - - [

¶ [*Ina*] *Abi* UD.6.KAM *Ninsianna* *ina ṣīt šamši innamir: zunnū ina šamê*

GÁL.MEŠ *ub-bu-tu* GÁL-ši EN UD.10.KAM šá ITI.BÁR ina ^{d}UTU.È DU-az
C - MEŠ - - - - *ϕ* 2 - - - - - - - - - - - - - - - -
H - ME - - - - - - 5' - U[D
L]⌜.⌝ - -

ibaššû ubbutu ibašši; adi UD.10.KAM *ša Nisanni ina ṣīt šamši izzaz*

UD.11.KAM šá ITI.BÁR i-tab-bal-ma 3 ITI ina AN-e ZAL-ma UD.11.KAM šá
C - - - - - - - - - - - - - 3 - - - - - - - - - - - - - -
H 18'] - -
L - - - - - - - [6'

UD.11.KAM *ša Nisanni itabbalma 3 arḫī ina šamê uḫḫaramma* UD.11.KAM *ša*

ITI.ŠU ^{d}Nin-si$_{4}$-an-na ina ^{d}UTU.ŠÚ.A SAR-ma SAL.KÚR.ME ina KUR GÁL.ME
C - - - - - - - - - - - - - - - - - 4 - - - - - - - - -
H - - - - - - - - - - - - - - [
L a]n - - - - - - - - - - SA[L
M 1'[

Du'ūzi Ninsianna ina ereb šamši inappaḫma: nukurātu ina māti ibaššâ

EBUR KUR SI.SÁ
C - - - -
H]
L]
M] - - -

ebūr māti iššir.

27 [DIŠ ina] ITI.KIN UD.7.KAM ^{d}Nin-si$_4$-an-na ina ^{d}UTU.ŠÚ.A IGI EBUR KUR SI.SÁ ŠÀ
C 5 [ ] -
H 19'[ ] - - - -
L 7' [ ]- - - - - - - - - - [
M 2' [
¶ [*Ina*] *Ulūli* UD.7.KAM *Ninsianna ina ereb šamši innamir: ebūr māti iššir libbi*

KUR DÙG-ab EN UD.11.KAM šá ITI.GUD ina ^{d}UTU.ŠÚ.A DU-az UD.12.KAM šá
C - - - 6 -
H - - - - - - - - - [
L 8'
M IT]I - - - - - - - - - 3' [
māti iṭâb; adi UD.11.KAM *ša Ajari ina ereb šamši izzaz* UD.12.KAM *ša*

ITI.GUD* i-tab-bal-ma 7 UD-mi ina AN-e uḫ-ḫa-ram-ma UD.19.KAM šá ITI.GUD
C - - -- - - - 7 7 UD-mi - - - - - - - - - - - - - - -
H 20' G]UD
L] - - - - - UD.7.KAM [
M
Ajari itabbalma 7 ūmī ina šamê uḫḫaramma UD.19.KAM *ša Ajari*

^{d}Nin-si$_4$-an-na ina ^{d}UTU.È SAR-ma SAL.KÚR.MEŠ ina KUR GÁL.MEŠ
C - - - - - - 8 - - - - - - - - - - MEŠ - - - MEŠ
H - - - - - - - - - - - - [ ]
L 9' n]a - - - - - - [ ]
M n]a - - - - - - - - - - - ME - - - ME
Ninsianna ina ṣīt šamši inappaḫma: nukurātu ina māti ibaššâ.

*Day of last visibility I 10 in *Iqqur īpuš*, see Labat Calendrier p. 259.

28 [DIŠ ina] ITI.DU$_6$ UD.8.KAM ^{d}Nin-si$_4$-an-na ina ^{d}UTU.È IGI.DU$_8$ SAL.KÚR.MEŠ ina
C [9] [ ] -
H [21'] [ ]
L [10'] [ ] - - - - - - - - - - [
M [4'] [
¶ [*Ina*] *Tašrīti* UD.8.KAM *Ninsianna* *ina ṣīt šamši innamir: nukurātu* *ina*

KUR GÁL.ME EBUR KUR SI.SÁ EN UD.12.KAM šá ITI.SIG$_4$ ina ^{d}UTU.È
C - - ME - - - - [10] - - - - - - - - - - - - -
H - - MEŠ - - [ ] [22'] (traces)
L [11']
M E]N - - - - - - - - - - -
māti ibaššâ ebūr māti iššir; adi UD.12.KAM *ša Simāni ina ṣīt šamši*

DU-az UD.13.KAM šá ITI.SIG$_4$ i-tab-bal-ma 3 ITI ina AN-e uḫ-ḫa-ram-ma
C - - - - - - - - - - - - - - [11] - - - - - - - - - - -
H
L] - - - - - - - - - [[12']
M - ϕ [5'] [
izzaz UD.13.KAM *ša Simāni itabbalma 3 arḫī ina šamê uḫḫaramma*

UD.13.KAM šá ITI.KIN ^{d}Nin-si$_4$-an-na ina ^{d}UTU.ŠÚ.A SAR-ma EBUR KUR
C - - - - - - - - - - - [12] - - - - - - - - - - -
H
L n]a - - - - - - - - - E[BUR
M] - - - - - - - [6'] [
UD.13.KAM *ša Ulūli Ninsianna ina ereb šamši inappaḫma: ebūr māti*

SI.SÁ ŠÀ KUR DÙG-ab
C - - - - - - - -
H
L]
M] - - - - -
iššir libbi māti iṭâb.

29 [DIŠ ina] ITI.APIN UD.9.KAM ^{d}Nin-si$_4$-an-na ina ^{d}UTU.ŠÚ.A IGI KUR SAL.KALA.GA
C [13] [ ] - [AP]IN - - - - - - - - - - - - - - - - - - -
L [13'] [ ] - - - - - - - - [
M [7'] [
¶ *[Ina] Araḫsamna* UD.9.KAM *Ninsianna ina ereb šamši innamir: māta dannatu*

DIB-bat EN UD.n.KAM šá ITI.ŠU ina ^{d}UTU.ŠÚ.A DU-az UD.14.KAM šá ITI.ŠU
C - - [14] - ⌜-⌝[ ] - - - - - - - - - - - - - - - - - - -
L [14']]
M x]+2 -
iṣabbat; adi UD.13.KAM *ša Du'ūzi ina ereb šamši izzaz* UD.14.KAM *ša Du'ūzi*

i-tab-bal-ma UD.7.KAM ina AN-e uḫ-ḫa-ram-ma UD.21.KAM šá ITI.ŠU ^{d}Nin-si$_4$-an-na
C - - - - - [15] - - - - ⌜- -⌝ - - - - - - - - - - - - - - - - -
L - - - - - - - - - [
M [8'] [n]a
itabbalma 7 ūmī ina šamê uḫḫaramma UD.21.KAM *ša Du'ūzi Ninsianna*

ina ^{d}UTU.È SAR-ma SAL.KÚR.MEŠ ina KUR GÁL.MEŠ EBUR KUR SI.SÁ
C [16] -
L [15']] - - - - M[EŠ]
M - - - - - - - - - - - - - - [ ] - -
ina ṣīt šamši inappaḫma: nukurātu ina māti ibaššâ ebūr māti iššir.

---

30 [DIŠ] ina ITI.GAN UD.10.KAM ^{d}Nin-si$_4$-an-na ina ^{d}UTU.È IGI SU.KÚ ŠE u IN.NU
C [17] [ ] -
M [9'] [ ] - - - - -
¶ *Ina Kislimi* UD.10.KAM *Ninsianna ina ṣīt šamši innamir: ḫušaḫḫi še'i u tibni*

ina KUR GÁL-ši EN UD.14.KAM šá ITI.NE ina ^{d}UTU.È DU-az UD.15.KAM šá
C - - - - [18] - - - - - - - - - - - - - - - - - - -
M - - - [-] [10'] [
ina māti ibašši; adi UD.14.KAM *ša Abi ina ṣīt šamši izzaz* UD.15.KAM *ša*

ITI.NE i-tab-bal-ma ITI 3 ina AN-e uḫ-ḫa-ram-ma UD.15.KAM šá ITI.APIN
C - - - - - - - [19] - - - - - - - - - - - - - - -
M I]TI - - - - m[a] [11'] [
Abi itabbalma 3 arḫī ina šamê uḫḫaramma UD.15.KAM *ša Araḫsamna*

^{d}Nin-si$_4$-an-na ina ^{d}UTU.ŠÚ.A SAR-ma EBUR KUR SI.SÁ
C - - - - - [20] - - - - - - - - - - - - -
M a]n - - - - - - - - - - - S[I -]
Ninsianna ina ṣīt šamši inappaḫma: ebūr māti iššir.

31 DIŠ ina ITI.AB UD.11.KAM ^{d}Nin-si$_4$-an-na ina ^{d}UTU.ŠÚ.A IGI EBUR KUR SI.SÁ EN
C 21 - 22 -
M r.1 [
¶ *Ina Ṭebēti* UD.11.KAM *Ninsianna ina ereb šamši innamir: ebūr māti iššir; adi*

UD.15.KAM šá ITI.KIN ina ^{d}UTU.ŠÚ.A DU-az UD.16.KAM šá ITI.KIN i-tab-bal-ma
C -
M] - - - - - - - - - - - a[z] 2 [
UD.15.KAM *ša Ulūli ina ereb šamši izzaz* UD.16.KAM *ša Ulūli itabbalma*

UD.7.KAM ina AN-e uḫ-ḫa-ram-ma UD.23.KAM šá ITI.KIN ^{d}Nin-si$_4$-an-na ina
C 23 - 24 -
M K]IN - - - - - - -
7 ūmī ina šamê uḫḫaramma UD.23.KAM *ša Ulūli Ninsianna ina*

^{d}UTU.È SAR-ma EBUR KUR SI.SÁ ŠÀ [KUR] DÙG.GA
C - - - KUR - - - - - - [ ] - -
M - - - SAR - - K[UR]
ṣīt šamši inappaḫma: ebūr māti iššir libbi [māti] iṭâb.

---

32 DIŠ ina ITI.ÁŠ UD.12.KAM ^{d}Nin-si$_4$-an-na ina ^{d}UTU.È IGI EBUR KUR [SI].SÁ EN
C 25 - [ ]⸢-⸣ 26 -
M 3 [
¶ *Ina Šabāṭi* UD.12.KAM *Ninsianna ina ṣīt šamši innamir: ebūr māti iššir; adi*

UD.16.KAM šá ITI.DU$_6$ ina ^{d}UTU.È DU-az UD.n.KAM šá ITI.DU$_6$ T[ÙM-ma]
C - - - - - - - - - - - - - - - 17 - - - - T[ÙM]
M] - - - - - - - - - - - ø - 16 - - - D[U$_6$]
UD.16.KAM *ša Tašrīti ina ṣīt šamši izzaz* UD.17.KAM *ša Tašrīti itabbal[ma]*

3 ITI ina AN-e uḫ-ḫa-ram-ma UD.17.KAM šá ITI.AB ^{d}Nin-si$_4$-an-na ina
C 27 - [ ] 28 -
M 4 [ ] - -
3 arḫī ina šamê uḫḫaramma UD.17.KAM *ša Ṭebēti Ninsianna ina*

^{d}UTU.ŠÚ.A SAR-ma EBUR KUR SI.SÁ
C - - - - - - - E[BUR]
M - - - - - - - - - - -
ereb šamši inappaḫma: ebūr māti iššir.

33 DIŠ ina ITI.ŠE UD.13.KAM ^{d}Nin-si$_4$-an-na ina ^{d}UTU.ŠÚ.A IGI LUGAL.MEŠ [ ]

C [29] - M[EŠ]

M [5] [

¶ *Ina Addari* UD.13.KAM *Ninsianna ina ereb šamši innamir: šarrāni* [ ];

EN UD.16.KAM šá ITI.APIN ina ^{d}UTU.ŠÚ.A DU-az UD.n.KAM šá ITI.APIN

C[30] - - - - - - - - - - - - - - - - - 16 - - - -

M 1]6 - - - - - - - - - - - ϕ [6][

adi UD.16.KAM *ša Araḫsamna ina ereb šamši izzaz* UD.17.KAM *ša Araḫsamna*

[TÙM-ma] UD.7.KAM ina AN-e uḫ-ḫa-ram-ma UD.25.KAM šá ITI.APIN

C [ ] [31] - - - - - - - - - - - - - - - - - - -

M] - - - - - - - - -

[*itabbalma*] *7 ūmī ina šamê uḫḫaramma* UD.25.KAM *ša Araḫsamna*

^{d}Nin-si$_4$-an-na ina ^{d}UTU.È SAR-ma KUR SAL.KALA.GA DIB-bat

C - - - a[n] [32] - - - - - - - - - - - - - [ ]

M - - - - - [7][KU]R - - - - - - -

N[1] (illegible traces)

Ninsianna ina ṣīt šamši inappaḫma: māta dannatu iṣabbat.

S$_2$ 12 ki-iṣ-ru ta-mu-ra-tum šá ^{d}Nin-si$_4$-an-na GABA.RI KÁ.DINGIR.RA^{ki}

C [33] - [ ]

M [8] [ ] - - - - - - - -

N [2'] [ ] - - - [ ]

B [r.1'] [ ] -

12 kiṣrū tāmurātu ša Ninsianna gabarī Bābili.

---

34 DIŠ ina ITI.KIN.2.KAM UD.1.KAM ^{d}Nin-si$_4$-an-na ina ^{d}UTU.ŠÚ.A it-[bal] UD.n.KAM ina
B 2' [
C 34 - [ ] 35 - 15 - -
M 9 [ ]16 - -
N 3' [KA]M - - - - - - - - - ⌈-⌉ [ ] 4' [
¶ *Ina Ulūli arkî* UD.1.KAM *Ninsianna ina ereb šamši it[bal] n ūmi ina*

AN-e uḫ-ḫa-ram-ma ina ITI.KIN.2.KAM UD.n.KAM ^{d}Nin-si$_4$-an-[na] ina ^{d}UTU.È
B]-ḫa-ram-ma 3' [
C - - ZAL -ma - - - - - - 17 - - - - - [ ] 36 - - - -
M - - uḫ-ḫa-ram-ma - - - - - - ḫi-pí eš-šú 10 [
N] ZAL -ma - - - - - - 14 - -N[in] 5' [
šamê uḫḫaramma ina Ulūli arkî UD.n.KAM *Ninsianna ina ṣīt šamši*

IGI GÁN.ZI SI.SÁ MU SAL ina KUR SUD-ti GÁL: ina É.GAL GU.LA
B] - - ⌈- -⌉ ϕ ϕ ϕ ϕ ϕ ϕ ϕ ϕ ϕ ϕ ϕ ϕ ϕ
C - ϕ ϕ ϕ ϕ - - - - - - - - - - - - [ ]
M SU]D - - - - - - - - -
N] - - - ⌈-⌉ [ ]
innamir: mērešu iššir . . . ina māti rūqti ibašši . . .

---

35 DIŠ ina ITI.SIG$_4$ UD.25.KAM ^{d}Nin-si$_4$-an-na ina ^{d}UTU.È it-bal 2 ITI UD.n.KAM ina
B 4' [ ]
C 37 - - - - - - - - - - - - - - - - - ba[l] 38 - - - 6 - -
M 11 [b]al - - - 16 - -
N 6' [ ] - - - - - - - - - - -[7'
¶ *Ina Simāni* UD.25.KAM *Ninsianna ina ṣīt šamši itbal 2 arḫī n ūmī ina*

AN-e uḫ-ḫa-ram-ma ina ITI.KIN UD.n.KAM ^{d}Nin-si$_4$-an-na ina
B - - uḫ-ḫa-[5'
C - - ZAL- ma - - - -24 [ ] 39 - - - - - -
M - - uḫ-ḫa-ram-ma 12 [ ]
N ZA]L- ma - - - -14 - UD.[x].KAM ⌈UD?⌉ [
šamê uḫḫaramma ina Ulūli UD.n.KAM *Ninsianna ina*

^{d}UTU.ŠÚ.A IGI ŠÀ KUR DÙG-ab
B] - -
C - - - - - - - - - -
M - - - - - - - - - -
N]
ereb šamši innamir: libbi māti iṭâb.

36 DIŠ ina ITI.BÁR UD.n.KAM ^{d}Nin-si$_{4}$-an-na ina ^{d}UTU.ŠÚ.A it-bal UD.7.KAM
B 6' [
C 40 - - - - - 27 - - - - - - - - - - - - - - - 41 - - -
M 13 [ ] ⸢ - ⸣
N 8' [ ] ⸢ - ⸣ 27 - UD.28.KA[M 9'
¶ *Ina Nisanni* UD.n.KAM *Ninsianna ina ereb šamši itbal 7 ūmī*

ina AN-e uḫ-ḫa-ram-ma ina ITI.GUD UD.3.KAM ^{d}Nin-si$_{4}$-an-na ina [^{d}UTU.È]
B] - - - - - 7' [
C - 42 - [ ]
M [ ] - - - - - - - 14[
N] - - - - - - [
ina šamê uḫḫaramma ina Ajari UD.3.KAM *Ninsianna ina [ṣīt šamši]*

IGI SAL.KÚR.ME ina KUR GÁL.ME EBUR KUR SI.SÁ
B] - - ⸢ - - ⸣
C - - - - - - - - ME - - - -
M]MEŠ - - - ⸢ - ⸣
N]
innamir: nukurātu ina māti ibaššâ ebūr māti iššir.

---

37 [DIŠ ina ITI.MN UD.n.KAM] ^{d}Nin-si$_{4}$-an-na ina ^{d}UTU.È it-bal [2 ITI ina AN-e
B 8' [
C 43 [ ] - - - - - - - - - - - - - 44[
N 10'[11'
¶ *[Ina Ṭebēti* UD.28.KAM] *Ninsianna ina ṣīt šamši itbal [2 arḫī ina šamê*

uḫ-ḫa] -ram-ma [ina] ITI.ŠE UD.28.KAM ^{d}Nin-si$_{4}$-an-na ina [^{d}UTU.ŠÚ.A IGI]
B] - - 9'[
C ZAL -ma] *ϕ* - - - - - - - - - - - 45[ ]
N] - - - - - - - - [
uḫḫa] ramma ina Addari UD.28.KAM *Ninsianna ina [ereb šamši innamir] :*

LUGAL ana LUGAL LÚ.NE KIN-ár
B]
C - - - - - - -
N]
šarru ana šarri ṣalta išappar.

S_3

C ^{46}[ ] x x [ ] ki-i KA LIBIR.RA-šu ^{47}[ ] (traces)

kî pī labīrišu

S_4

N $^{12'}$[ ] ZU AM AM [ ] $^{13'}$[ ] TA ki-iṣ-ri x [ ]

S_5

K $^{5'}$ [ ] ^{d}Nin-si$_4$-an-na a-ḫu-t[um]

---

38 DIŠ ina ITI.BÁR ^{d}Nin-si$_4$-an-na UD.8.KAM ina ^{d}UTU.È [it-bal] 5 ITI.MEŠ UD.n.KAM

T ^{1} - - - - - - - - - - - - - - - -[ ] ^{2} - - - - 17 -

P $^{3'}$ [IT]I - - - - - - - - [$^{4'}$

K $^{6'}$ [ ] - - - - - - - - - ⸢- - - - - -⸣ [ ]$^{7'}$⸢x⸣ i - - ϕ - 18 -

¶ *Ina Nisanni Ninsianna* UD.8.KAM *ina ṣīt šamši [itbal] 5 arḫī n ūmī*

ina AN-e uḫ-ḫi-ram-ma ina ITI.KIN UD.n.KAM ^{d}Nin-si$_4$-an-na ina ^{d}[UTU.ŠÚ.A

T - - [ ]^{3} - - - - 25 - - - - - - - - -[

P]$^{4'}$ - - - - 24 - - - - - - - [

K - - - ZAL-ma - - ⸢- ⸣ [

ina šamê uḫḫiramma ina Ulūli UD.n.KAM *Ninsianna ina [ereb šamši*

IGI.DU$_8$ ŠÀ KUR DÙG-ab]

T]

P]

K]

innamir: libbi māti iṭâb].

39	DIŠ	ina	ITI.BÁR	^{d}Nin-si$_{4}$-an-na	UD.n.KAM	ina	^{d}UTU.[ŠÚ.A	it-bal]	UD.6.KAM	ina	AN-e
T 4	-	-	- -	- - - - - -	- 26 -	-	-[	]	5 - - -	-	- -
P 5'	[		BÁ]R	- - - - -	- 26 -	-	-[				
K 8'	[	]	- -	- - - - - - -	- 27 -	-	- - È	[			
¶	*Ina*	*Nisanni*		*Ninsianna*	UD.n.KAM	*ina*	*ereb šamši*	*itbal*	UD.6.KAM	*ina*	*šamê*

	uḫ-ḫi-ram-ma	ina	ITI.GUD	UD.3.KAM	^{d}Nin-si$_{4}$-an-na	ina	^{d}UTU.È	IGI-ir
T	- - - - -	- [				]6 -	- - È	- -
P	6'		IT]I -	- - -	φ φ φ φ φ	-	- - È	- -
K	9'		] -	- - -	- - - - - -	-	- - ⸢ŠÚ.A⸣ [	
	uḫḫiramma	*ina*	*Ajari*	UD.3.KAM	*Ninsianna*	*ina*	*ṣīt šamši*	*innamir:*

	nu-ku-ra-a-[tum	ina	KUR	GÁL.ME	EBUR	KUR	SI.SÁ]
T	- - - ⸢-⸣ [						]
P	[						]
K							]
	nukurā[tu	*ina*	*māti*	*ibaššâ*	*ebūr*	*māti*	*iššir].*

40	DIŠ	ina	ITI.GUD	^{d}Nin-si$_{4}$-an-na	UD.2.KAM	ina	^{d}UTU.ŠÚ.A	[it-bal]	UD.n.KAM	ina	AN-e
T 7	-	-	- -	[ ]- - -	- - - -	-	[	]	8 - [ ]⸢- ⸣	-	- -
P 7'	[		G]UD	- - - - -	- - -	-	- - - [		8']⸢x⸣ -	-	- [
K 10'	[		IT]I -	- - - - - -	- - -	-	- - ⸢- -⸣	[			
¶	*Ina*	*Ajari*		*Ninsianna*	UD.2.KAM	*ina*	*ereb šamši*	*[itbal]*	*n ūmī*	*ina*	*šamê*

	uḫ-ḫi-ram-ma	[ina	ITI.]GUD	UD.n.KAM	ina	^{d}UTU.È	IGI-ir	ŠÈG	u
T	- - - -	[			9	] - -	- -	-	-
P									
K	11'		G]UD	UD.28.KAM: UD.18.KAM -	- - -	- φ	-	[	
	uḫḫiramma	*[ina]*	*Ajari*	UD.n.KAM	*ina*	*ṣīt šamši*	*innamir:*	*zunnu*	*u*

	A.[KAL	GÁL.ME	EBUR	KUR	SI.SÁ]
T	⸢-⸣ [				]
P					]
K					]
	mī[lu	*ibaššû*	*ebūr*	*māti*	*iššir].*

41 DIŠ ina [ITI].GUD ^{d}Nin-si$_4$-an-na UD.5.KAM ina ^{d}UTU.ŠÚ.A [it-bal] UD.n.KAM ina
T ^{10} - - [ ] - - - - - - - - - [^{11}]⸢7⸣ - -
K $^{12'}$[G]UD - - - - - - - - - - - - - - [
V $^{i\ 1'}$[ ] $^{2'}$ ITI.6.K[AM*
¶ *Ina Ajari Ninsianna* UD.5.KAM *ina ereb šamši* [*itbal*] *7 ūmī ina*

AN-e uḫ-ḫi-ram-m[a ina ITI.GUD UD.12.KAM] ^{d}Nin-si$_4$-an-na ina ^{d}UTU.È IGI-ir
T - - - - - m[a ^{12}] - - - - - - - ⸢-⸣ [
K $^{13'}$ K]AM - - - - - - - - ⸢x⸣ [
V] $^{3'}$ ina ITI.SIG$_4$ [ ] $^{4'}$⸢- - - -⸣ [
šamê uḫḫiramma ina MN UD.12.KAM *Ninsianna ina ṣīt šamši innamir:*

EBUR KUR SI.SÁ
T]
K]
V]
ebūr māti iššir.

---

42 DIŠ ina ITI.SIG$_4$ ^{d}Nin-si$_4$-an-na UD.n.[KAM ina ^{d}UTU.È it-bal n ITI] UD.n.KAM
T ^{13}[ ] ⸢- -⸣[ ] - - ⸢-⸣ [
K $^{14'}$[ ] - - - - - x[
V $^{5'}$ - - - - MUL [Dil-bat] $^{6'}$ ina UD**.1.KAM UD.9[
¶ *Ina Simāni Ninsianna* UD.n.KAM *ina ṣīt šamši itbal n arḫī n ūmī*

[ina AN-e] uḫ-ḫi-ram-[ma ina ITI.KIN UD]n.KAM ina ^{d}UTU.ŠÚ.A [IGI
T
K $^{15'}$ x]+5 - - - - [
V] $^{7'}$ - - ra [$^{8'}$] ⸢-⸣ - - - [
ina šamê uḫḫiram[*ma ina Ulūli* UD].n.KAM *ina ereb šamši* [*innamir:*

ŠÀ KUR DÙG-ab]
T]
K]
V]
libbi māti iṭâb].

---

*ITI.6.K[AM] (V) error for UD.6.KAM.

**UD (V) error for ITI.

43 [DIŠ ina ITI.ŠU] ^{d}Nin-si$_4$-an-na [UD.n.KAM ina ^{d}UTU.È it-bal n ITI UD.n.KAM ina
V $^{9'}$[ ] MUL [Dil-bat]$^{10'}$(traces)
¶ [*ina Du'ūzi*] *Ninsianna* [UD.n.KAM *ina ṣīt šamši itbal n* ITI *n ūmī ina*

AN-e uḫ-ḫi-[ram-ma ina ITI.MN UD.n.KAM] ina ^{d}UTU.[ŠÚ.A IGI]
V $^{11'}$- ḫ[i] $^{12'}$- -UT[U]
šamê] *uḫḫi*[*ramma ina* MN UD.n.KAM] *ina* [*ereb*] *šamši* [*innamir* . . .]

---

44 DIŠ ina ITI.ŠU [^{d}Nin-si$_4$-an-na UD.n.KAM ina ^{d}UTU.È] it-bal [UD.n.KAM ina AN-e
V $^{13'}$- - - - [ ] $^{14'}$- b[al
Q $^{1'}$[
¶ *Ina Du'ūzi* [*Ninsianna* UD.n.KAM *ina ṣīt šamši*] *itbal* [*n ūmī ina šamê*

uḫ-ḫi-ram-ma] ina ITI.MN [UD.n.KAM] ina ^{d}UTU.ŠÚ.A [IGI]
V]$^{15'}$- -Š[U]$^{16'}$- -UT[U]
Q Š]Ú- [ ]
uḫḫiramma] *ina* MN [UD.n.KAM] *ina ereb šamši* [*innamir* . . .]

---

45 DIŠ ina ITI.[NE ^{d}Nin-si$_4$-an-na UD.n.KAM ina] ^{d}UTU.ŠÚ.A it-bal [UD.n.KAM ina AN-e]
V $^{17'}$- - - [ ]$^{18'}$- [ ]
Q $^{2'}$[ ] - - - - - b[al
¶ *Ina* [*Abi Ninsianna* UD.n.KAM *ina*] *ereb šamši itbal* [*n ūmī ina šamê*]

uḫ-[ḫi-ram-ma ina ITI.MN UD.n.KAM ina ^{d}UTU.È IGI] ŠÈG.MEŠ ina AN-e
V$^{19'r.1}$[ ]$^{20'-21'}$(traces)
Q $^{3'}$] - - - A[N
A$^{r.1'}$[
uḫ[*ḫiramma ina* MN UD.n.KAM *ina ṣīt šamši innamir*] : *zunnū ina šamê*

[A.KAL.MEŠ ina IDIM GÁL.MEŠ] EBUR KUR SI.SÁ
A EB]UR - - -
Q]
[*mīlū ina nagbī ibaššû*] *ebūr māti iššir.*

46 [DIŠ ina ITI.NE ^{d}Nin-si$_4$-an-na UD.n.KAM] ina ^{d}UTU.È it-bal [n ITI UD.n.KAM ina
A 2' [
Q 4' [ ] - - - - - b[al
¶ [*Ina Abi Ninsianna* UD.n.KAM] *ina ṣīt šamši itbal* [*n arḫī n ūmī ina*

AN-e] uḫ-ḫi-ram-ma [ina ITI. MN UD.n.KAM ina ^{d}UTU.ŠÚ].A IGI-ir ŠÈG.MEŠ
A] - - - - 3' [
Q 5'] - - - - -
šamê] *uḫḫiramma* [*ina* MN UD.n.KAM *ina*] *ereb šamši innamir: zunnū*

[ina KUR GÁL].MEŠ ub-bu-tu GAR-an
A ME]Š - - - - -
Q [ ]
[*ina māti ibaššû*] *ubbutu iššakkan.*

---

47 [DIS ina ITI.NE ^{d}Nin-si$_4$-an-na UD.n].KAM ina ^{d}UTU.È it-bal 2 [ITI UD.n.KAM ina]
A 4' [ ]
Q 6' [ ] - - - - - - - 1 +[
¶ [*Ina Abi Ninsianna* UD.n].KAM *ina ṣīt šamši itbal 2* [*arḫī n ūmī ina*]

AN-e uḫ-ḫi-ram-ma [ina ITI.MN UD.n.KAM] ina ^{d}UTU.ŠÚ.A IGI-ir ŠÈG.MEŠ
A - - - - - - - 5' [ ] - - - - - - i[r
Q 7'] - - -
šamê uḫḫiramma [*ina* MN UD.n.KAM] *ina ereb šamši innamir: zunnū*

ina KUR GÁL.MEŠ ub-bu-tu GAR-an
A] - - - - - - -
Q - - [ ]
ina māti ibaššû ubbutu iššakkan.

48 DIŠ ina ITI.KIN ^{d}Nin-si$_4$-an-na UD.23.KAM ina ^{d}UTU.ŠÚ.A it-bal UD.20.KAM ina AN-e
A 6' -
Q 8' [ ] - - - - - - i[t
¶ *Ina Ulūli Ninsianna* UD.23.KAM *ina ereb šamši itbal 20 ūmī ina šamê*

uḫ-ḫi-ram-ma ina ITI.DU$_6$ UD.13.KAM ina ^{d}UTU.È IGI-ir nu-kúr-a-tum ina KUR
A - - - - - 7' -
Q 9'] - - [
uḫḫiramma ina Tašrīti UD.13.KAM *ina ṣīt šamši innamir: nukurātu ina māti*

GÁL.MEŠ EBUR KUR SI.SÁ
A - - - - - -
Q]
ibaššâ ebūr māti iššir.

---

49 DIŠ ina ITI.KIN ^{d}Nin-si$_4$-an-na UD.26.KAM ina ^{d}UTU.ŠÚ.A it-bal UD.12.KAM ina AN-e
A 8' -
¶ *Ina Ulūli Ninsianna* UD.26.KAM *ina ereb šamši itbal* UD.12.KAM *ina šamê*

uḫ-ḫi-ram-ma ina ITI.KIN.2.KAM UD.8.KAM ina ^{d}UTU.È IGI ŠÀ KUR DÙG-ab
A - - - - - - 9' - - - - - - - - - - - - - - - - ŠÀ* -
uḫḫiramma ina Ulūli arkî UD.8.KAM *ina ṣīt šamši innamir: libbi māti iṭâb.*

---

50 DIŠ ina ITI.DU$_6$ ^{d}Nin-si$_4$-an-na UD.11.KAM ina ^{d}UTU.ŠÚ.A it-bal 1 ITI UD.17.KAM
A 10' -
¶ *Ina Tašrīti Ninsianna* UD.11.KAM *ina ereb šamši itbal 1* ITI *17 ūmī*

ina AN-e uḫ-ḫi-ram-ma ina ITI.APIN UD.28.KAM ^{d}Nin-si$_4$-an-na ina ^{d}UTU.È
A - - - - - - - - 11' - - - - - - - - - - - - - - - -
ina šamê uḫḫiramma ina Araḫsamna UD.28.KAM *Ninsianna ina ṣīt šamši*

IGI-ir ŠÈG.ME ina KUR GÁL.ME ub-bu-tu GAR-an
A - - - - - - - - - - - - - - -
innamir: zunnū ina māti ibaššû ubbutu iššakkan.

---

*ŠÀ-*ab* (A) error for DÙG-*ab*.

51 DIŠ ina ITI.APIN ^{d}Nin-si$_{4}$-an-na UD.28.KAM ina ^{d}UTU.ŠÚ.A it-bal UD.5.KAM ina AN-e
A 12' -
¶ *Ina Araḫsamna Ninsianna* UD.28.KAM *ina ereb šamši itbal 5 ūmī ina šamê*

ZAL-ma ina ITI.GAN [UD.3.KAM] ina ^{d}UTU.È IGI-ir SU.KÚ ŠE u IN.NU
A - - - 13' ⌜ - ⌝ [ ] - - - - - - - - - - - - -
uḫḫiramma ina Kislimi [UD.3.KAM] *ina ṣīt šamši innamir: ḫušaḫḫi še'i u tibni*

ina KUR GÁL
A - - -
ina māti ibašši.

---

52 [DIŠ ina ITI.APIN ^{d}Nin-si$_{4}$-an-na UD.11.KAM ina ^{d}UTU].È it-bal 2 ITI UD.8.KAM ina
A 14'[ ] - - - - - - - - - -
¶ [*Ina Araḫsamna Ninsianna* UD.11.KAM *ina*] *ṣīt* [*šamši*] *itbal 2 arḫī 8 ūmī ina*

AN-e ZAL-ma ina ITI.AB UD.19.KAM ina ^{d}UTU.ŠÚ.A IGI EBUR KUR SI.SÁ
A -
šamê uḫḫiramma ina Ṭebēti UD.19.KAM *ina ereb šamši innamir: ebūr māti iššir.*

---

53 [DIŠ ina ITI.APIN ^{d}Nin-si$_{4}$-an-na UD.n].KAM ina ^{d}UTU.È it-bal 2 ITI UD.8.KAM ina
A 15'[i]t - - - - - - - -
O 1' [ ] - - - - - ⌜ - - ⌝ - - [
¶ [*Ina Araḫsamna Ninsianna* UD.n].KAM *ina ṣīt šamši itbal, 2 arḫī 8 ūmī ina*

AN-e uḫ-ḫi-ram-ma [ina ITI.A]B UD.16.KAM ina ^{d}UTU.ŠÚ.A IGI-ir EBUR KUR
A - - - - - - [- - A]B - - - - - - - - - - - -
O 2'] ⌜ - - ⌝ - - - ϕ [
šamê uḫḫiramma [*ina*] *Ṭebēti* UD.16.KAM *ina ereb šamši innamir: ebūr māti*

SI.SÁ
A - -
O]
iššir.

54	[DIŠ	ina	ITI.GAN	^{d}Nin-si_4-an-n]a	UD.12.KAM	ina	^{d}UTU.È	it-bal	2	ITI	UD.[n.KAM]	ina
A 16'	[				x+]1 -	-	- - -	it-bal	-	IT[I	]	-
O 3'	[			n]a	- 12 -	-	- - -	TÙM	-	-	- [	
J r.1'	[						-				]	⌈-
¶	[Ina		*Kislimi*	*Ninsian*]*na*	UD.12.KAM	*ina*	*ṣīt šamši*	*itbal*	*2*	*arḫī*	*n ūmī*	*ina*

	AN-e	uḫ-ḫi-ram-ma	[ina	ITI.ÁŠ	UD.16.KAM	ina]	^{d}UTU.ŠÚ.A	IGI-ir	EBUR	KUR
A	- -	uḫ-ḫi-ram-ma	17'[				]-	- -	-	[ ]
O			4'			]	- - - -	- -	[	
J	- -	ZAL-ma⌉	2'[						] -	-
	šamê	*uḫḫiramma*	[*ina*	*Šabāṭi*	UD.16.KAM	*ina*]	*ereb šamši innamir:*		*ebūr*	*māti*

	SI.SÁ
A	- -
O	]
J	- -
	iššir.

55	[DIŠ	ina	ITI.AB	^{d}Nin-si_4-an-n]a	UD.24.KAM	ina	^{d}UTU.ŠÚ.A	it-bal	1	ITI	UD.4.KAM
A 18'	[						] - - -	it-bal	< >	-	- - -
O 5'	[			n]a	- - ϕ	-	- - - -	TÙM	1	-	- [
J 3'	[										]
¶	[*Ina*		*Ṭebēti*	*Ninsian*]*na*	UD.24.KAM	*ina*	*ereb šamši*	*itbal*	*1*	ITI	*4 ūmī*

	ina	AN-e	ZAL-ma	ina	ITI.ÁŠ	UD.28.KAM	ina	^{d}UTU.È	IGI-ir	EBUR	KUR	SI.SÁ
A	-	- -	-	-	- -	- - -	-	- - -	- -	-	-	- -
O				6'			]	- - -	- ϕ	[		]
J	-	- -	-	- 4'[					]	-	-	- -
	ina	*šamê*	*uḫḫiramma*	*ina*	*Šabāṭi*	UD.28.KAM	*ina*	*ṣīt šamši*	*innamir:*	*ebūr*	*māti*	*iššir.*

56 [DIŠ ina ITI.AB ^{d}Nin-si$_{4}$-an-n]a UD.28.KAM ina ^{d}UTU.È it-bal 2 ITI ina AN-e
A 19' [ ] - - - - - it-bal - - - - - -
O 7' [n]a - - - - - [ ] - TÙM [
J 5' [IT]I - - -
¶ *[Ina Ṭebēti Ninsian]na* UD.28.KAM *ina ṣīt šamši itbal 2 arḫī ina šamê*

uḫ-ḫi-ram-ma [ina ITI.ŠE UD.28.KAM ina] ^{d}UTU.ŠÚ.A IGI-ir LUGAL ana
A uḫ-ḫi-ra[m-m]a 20'[ ] - - - -
O 8'] - - - - I[GI
J ZAL-ma 6' [ ] - -
U 1' [ ] - - [ ] 2'[
uḫḫiramma [ina Addari UD.28.KAM *ina] ereb šamši innamir: šarru ana*

LUGAL LÚ.NE KIN-ár
A - LÚ.NE - -
O]
J - SAL.KÚR - -
U LÚ.N]E - [ ]
šarri ṣalta išappar.

---

57 [DIŠ ina ITI.ÁŠ ^{d}Nin-si$_{4}$-an-na UD.n]KAM ina ^{d}UTU.ŠÚ.A it-bal UD.3.KAM ina AN-e
A 21'[ ] - - - - - - - - - - - - - - -
J 7' [ ]- - - - -
U 3' [ ] - - - - - 4'[
V ii 1'[ ] ⸢- - 12'[
¶ *[Ina Šabāṭi Ninsianna* UD.n].KAM *ina ereb šamši itbal 3 ūmī ina šamê*

ZAL-ma ina ITI.ÁŠ UD.n.KAM ina ^{d}UTU.È IGI ^{d}IM ŠÈG.MEŠ-šú ^{d}É-a IDIM-šu
A ZAL-ma - - - - 28 - 22'[I]M - - šú - - - - -
J ZAL-ma - - - - 18 - - - - - - - 8'[ ]
U IT]I - - 18 - 5' [Š]ÈG - šu ^{d}IM - -
V uḫ]-⸢ḫi-ra⸣-ma 3' [ ] - 4'[
uḫḫiramma ina Šabāṭi UD.n.KAM *ina ṣīt šamši innamir: Adad zunnēšu Ea nagbīšu*

ub-ba-lam LUGAL ana LUGAL SILIM.MA KIN-ár
A - - - - - - - - - - -
J - - - - - - - - - - -
U [6'] - - - -
V]5'[ ]
ubbalam šarru ana šarri salīma išappar.

58 [DIŠ ina ITI.ŠE ^{d}Nin-si$_4$-an-na UD.n].KAM ina ^{d}UTU.È it-bal 2 ITI UD.7.KAM ina

A 23'[ ] - - - - - - - - - - - - - -

J 9' [b]al - - - - - -

U 7' [ ] - - - - 8'[

V 6' [ ]⌜-⌝ - - 7'[

¶ [*ina Addari Ninsianna* UD.n]KAM *ina ṣīt šamši itbal 2 arḫī 7 ūmī ina*

AN-e uḫ-ḫi-ram-ma ina ITI.SIG$_4$ UD.4.KAM [ina] ^{d}UTU.ŠÚ.A IGI-ir

A - - uḫ-ḫi-ram-ma 24'[ ] - - - - - - -

J - ⌜- ZAL⌝-ma ⌜- -⌝ - - - - [ ]

U u]ḫ-ḫi-ram-ma [ ] ⌜- -⌝

V] uḫ-ḫi-ra-ma 8' [MU]L Dil-bat 9'[

šamê uḫḫiramma ina Simāni UD.4.KAM *(Dilbat) [ina] ereb šamši innamir:*

ŠUB-tim ERÍN ma-at-ti

A - ϕ - - - -

J - ϕ - - ⌜- -⌝

U [ ]

V t]im - - - -

miqitti ummàni matti.

---

59 [DIŠ ina ITI.ŠE ^{d}Nin-s]i$_4$-an-na [UD.10].KAM ina ^{d}UTU.ŠÚ.A it-bal UD.4.KAM ina

A 25'[s]i$_4$ - - ϕ ϕ ϕ - - - ŠÚ.A - - - - - - -

J 10'[ ] - - -

V 10'[ ] - - - - È 11'[ ]

¶ [*Ina Addari Nin*]*sianna* [UD.10].KAM *ina ereb šamši itbal 4 ūmī ina*

AN-e uḫ-ḫi-ram-ma ina ITI.ŠE UD.14.KAM ina ^{d}UTU.È IGI: ina AN IGI

A - - - - - - - 26'[ ] - - - - - -

J - - ZAL - - - - - - - - - - - - [

V - - 12'[KA]M [

šamê uḫḫiramma ina Addari UD.14.KAM *ina ṣīt šamši innamir:*

LUGAL ana LUGAL SILIM.MA KIN-ár KI.A SI.SÁ ŠÀ KUR DÙG-ab

A - - - - - - - - - - - - - - - -

J 11'] - - - - - - - - -

V]

šarru ana šarri salīma išappar ruṭibtu iššir libbi māti iṭâb.

S$_6$ [ ] ^{d}Nin-si$_4$-an-na a-ḫu-tum
A 27'[ ] - - - - - - - - -
J 12'[ ] - - -
[*21 kiṣrū*? *ša*] *Ninsianna* *aḫûtu*

S$_7$ 4? ki[ṣrū? ša ^{d}Ninsianna aḫûtu] TA ŠÀ! [ki-iṣ]-ri ta-a-a-ar-ta ina ŠÀ-bi i-šu-ú
B r.10'⌜-⌝ - [ ] (traces) 11' - BAR x-[ ]-
R 1' (traces) 2' [ ] - - - - - - - - - - - ⌜-⌝[ ]
4? *ki*[*ṣrū*? *ša* *Ninsianna* *aḫûtu* *ultu libbi kiṣ*]*ri* *tajarta* *ina* *libbi* *išû.*

---

60 DIŠ ina ITI.DU$_6$ ^{d}Nin-si$_4$-an-na UD.3.KAM ina ^{d}UTU.ŠÚ.A it-bal 1 ITI UD.7.KAM
B 12' - - - - -N[in] - - [
R 3' [ ] - - - - 3 - - - - - - - - - - - - - - -
N 14'[n]a - 11 ⌜-⌝ [ ] - - - - i[t
¶ *Ina* *Tašrīti* *Ninsianna* UD.3.KAM *ina* *ereb šamši* *itbal* *1* ITI *7* *ūmī*

[ina AN-e uḫ]-ḫa-ram-ma ina ITI.APIN UD.n.KAM ^{d}Nin-si$_4$-an-na [ina ^{d}UTU.È]
B] - - - 13' - - - - ⌜27⌝ - - - [
R [4'] - - - - - - - 28 - - - - - - - 5'[ ]
N 15']⌜-? ⌝ - - [
[*ina* *šamê* *uḫ*]*ḫaramma* *ina* *Araḫsamna* UD.n.KAM *Ninsianna* [*ina* *ṣit* *šamši*]

IGI ŠÈG.MEŠ ina KUR GÁL.MEŠ ub-bu-tu GAR-an
B] - - -
R - - - - - - - - - - - - - -
N]
innamir: *zunnū* *ina* *māti* *ibaššû* *ubbutu* *iššakkan.*

S$_8$ 2 ki-iṣ-ru šá ^{d}Nin-si$_4$-an-na a-ḫu-tum TA ŠÀ ki-iṣ-ri ta-a-a-ra-tum ina ŠÀ-bi i-šu-ú
B 14'- - - - - -Ni[n b]i - - ⌜-⌝
R 6' [ ] - ϕ - ⌜-⌝[ ]

Colophons

A (= Hunger Kolophone 469)

Rev. 28' [DIŠ MUL.SAG.ME.GAR ina še-er-ti ik-tu]-un LUGAL.MEŠ KÚR.MEŠ SILIM.MEŠ
DUB 1 UŠ 3 KAM DIŠ UD An ^{d}En-líl
29' [ ] x GIŠ ^{md}U+GUR-DIN-iṭ

End
28' "If Jupiter remains (in the sky) in the morning, enemy kings will become reconciled"
[= catchline of Tablet 64].
Tablet 63 of Enūma Anu Enlil.
29' [. . .] written by Nergal-uballiṭ.

B (= Hunger Kolophone 150)

Rev. 15' DIŠ MUL.SAG.ME.GAR ina še-er-ti i[k-tu-un LUGAL.MEŠ KÚR.MEŠ] SILIM.MEŠ
16' DUB 1 UŠ 2.ÀM.KAM.MA [DIŠ] [UD An] ^{d}En-líl 37.ÀM MU.B[I.IM]
17' [G]ABA.RI Ba-bi-i-li^{ki} [G]IM la-bi-ri-šú ša-ṭir-ma [È]
18' [Š]U ^{d}U+GUR-DU-uš DUMU LÚ.DUMU.DÙ AN [x]
19' [(x)] E^{ki} MU.AN.NA [x].KAM LÚGAL.GI.NA LUGAL [ ]

End
15' "If Jupiter remains (in the sky) in the morning, enemy kings will become reconciled"
[= catchline of Tablet 64].
16' Tablet 62 of Enūma Anu Enlil, it has 37 lines.
17' Copy of (a text from) Babylon, written according to its original and collated.
18' Written by Nergal-ēpuš, son of a "Free man" . . .
19' At Babylon, [x]th year of Sargon, king [of Assyria].

J

Rev. 13' [DUB . . . KAM DIŠ UD An ^{d}En-líl] NU AL.TIL
14' [ ] x MU.ME ḪUL.ME TA É.KUR È-am
15' [ ]-x-mu-še-zi-bu x [n]i$^{?}$ ^{m}DIN-su-^{d}EN
16' [ ] x GIŠ x [ ] (blank)

break

13' Tablet n of Enūma Anu Enlil, unfinished.
14' [. . .] evil years$^{?}$ will come out of Ekur (catchline of the "akītu-omens," see provisionally ACh Second Supplément 82 and Gadd, CT 40 p. 8 to pl. 38-40).
15' [. . .]-mušēzibu . . . Uballissu-Bēl
16' (remainder fragmentary).

R

Rev. 7' [DUB x].KAM UD An ^{d}En-líl [ ]
8' [ ] x ⌜SU⌝ x x x$^{hi-pí}$

break

7' Tablet n of Enūma Anu Enlil, [unfinished].
8' . . . broken.

Appendix A. Excerpt from EAE 63 in *Iqqur īpuš* (§ 104A)

K.3170 + 11719 + 14551

Omen 22 end: 1' [3 ITI ina AN-e ZAL-ma UD.8.KAM šá IT]I.ŠE ina ^{d}UTU.ŠÚ.A KUR-ma [LUGAL ana LUGAL SAL.KÚR KIN-ár]

Omen 23: 2' [DIŠ ina ITI.GUD UD].⌈3⌉.KAM ^{d}Nin-si$_{4}$-an-n[a ina ^{d}UTU.ŠÚ.A IGI]

3' [SAL.KÚR.MEŠ] ina KUR GÁL.MEŠ EN UD.7.KAM šá ITI.AB ina ^{d}UTU.ŠÚ.[A DU]

4' [UD.7.KA]M šá ITI.AB TÙM-ma UD.7.KAM ina AN ZAL-[m]a UD.14.KAM šá ITI.[AB]

5' [ina ^{d}U]TU.È KUR-ma EBUR KUR SI.SÁ ŠÀ KUR DÙG-ab

Omen 24: 6' [DIŠ ina ITI.SI]G$_{4}$ UD.4.KAM ^{d}Nin-si$_{4}$-an-na ina ^{d}⌈UTU⌉.È IGI RI.RI.GA ERÍN mat-ti

7' [EN U]D.7.KAM šá ITI.ÁŠ ina ^{d}UTU.È DU UD.8(or: 7).KAM šá ITI.ÁŠ TÙM-ma

8' [3] ITI.MEŠ ina AN-e ZAL-ma UD.12.KAM šá ITI.GUD ina ^{d}UTU.ŠÚ.A KUR-ma SAL.KÚR.ME ina KUR GÁL.ME

Omen 25: 9' [DIŠ ina] ITI.ŠU UD.5.KAM ^{d}Nin-si$_{4}$-an-na ina $^{[d]}$UTU.ŠÚ.A IGI SAL.KÚR.MEŠ ina KUR G[ÁL.MEŠ]

10' EBUR KUR SI.SÁ EN UD.9.KAM šá ITI.[Š]E ina ^{d}UTU.ŠÚ.A DU UD.10.KAM šá ITI.ŠE TÙM-m[a]

11' UD.7.KAM ina AN ZAL-ma UD.17.KAM šá I[TI].ŠE ina ^{d}UTU.È KUR-ma LUGAL ana LUGAL SAL.KÚR KIN-[ár]

Omen 26: 12' [DIŠ ina ITI].NE UD.6.KAM ^{d}Nin-si$_{4}$-an-na ina ^{d}UTU.È IGI ŠÈG.ME ina AN-e GÁL.ME

13' [ub-bu-t]u GÁL EN U[D.10.KAM šá ITI].BÁR ina ^{d}UTU.È DU

14' [UD.11.KAM šá ITI.BÁR TÙM-ma 3 ITI ina AN ZAL-m]a UD.11.KAM šá ITI.ŠU

15' [ina ^{d}UTU.ŠÚ.A KUR-ma SAL.KÚR.ME ina KUR GÁL.ME EBU]R KUR SI.SÁ

Omen 27: 16' [DIŠ ina ITI.KIN UD.2.KAM ^{d}Nin-si$_{4}$-an-na ina ^{d}UTU.ŠÚ.A IGI] EBUR KUR SI.SÁ

break

Appendix B. E BM 41498 = LBAT 1562

1' [. . . . . ina IT]I.ŠU(or: DU$_6$) UD.14.KAM
2' [(^{d}Nin-si$_4$-an-na) ina ^{d}UTU.È IGI.DU$_8$ LUGAL ana LUGA]L LÚ.NE KIN-ár

---

3' [DIŠ ina ITI.APIN UD.10.KAM ^{d}Nin-si$_4$-an-na ina ^{d}UTU].È it-bal 2 ITI UD.9.KAM
4' [ina AN-e ZAL-ma ina ITI.AB UD.19.KAM ina ^{d}UTU.ŠÚ].A IGI-ir EBUR KUR SI.SÁ

5' [DIŠ ina ITI.MN UD.n.KAM ^{d}Nin-si$_4$-an-na ina ^{d}UT]U.È ⸢it⸣-bal 2 ITI UD.1.KAM
6' [ina AN-e ZAL-ma ina ITI.MN UD.n.KAM ina ^{d}UTU.ŠÚ.A IGI-ir] EBUR KUR [SI.SÁ]

---

traces of one line

rev. 1' [ina AN]-e$^?$ [ZAL-ma]
2' [ina ITI.MN UD.n.KA]M ina ^{d}UTU.ŠÚ.A IGI-i[r] EŠ A [ ]

3' [DIŠ ina ITI.MN UD.n.KAM ^{d}Nin-si$_4$-an-n]a ina ^{d}UTU.ŠÚ.A i[t]-bal
4' [ina ^{d}UT]U.È IGI ŠÈG.MEŠ ina ⸢KUR⸣ [ ]
5' [ ] UR$^?$ MEŠ ḪUL$^?$ BI x [ ]
6' [DIŠ ina ITI.MN UD.n.KAM ^{d}Nin-si$_4$-an-na ina] ^{d}UTU.È i[t-bal . . .]
7' [ ] 30 [xx] UD 20 [. . .]
8' [i]t$^?$-bal UD.x.[
9' traces

Appendix C. K BM 34227 + 42033 = LBAT 1560 + 1561

1' traces

2' [ ].MEŠ ub-bu-tu GAR-an

3' [DIŠ ina ITI.Š]E? ^{d}Nin-si$_4$-an-na UD.24.KAM [ ]

4' [ina AN]-⌜e⌝ ZAL-ma ina ITI.ÁŠ UD.28.KAM ^{d}N[in-si$_4$-an-na . . .]

5'- 15' = S_5, Omens 38-42.

The apodosis of the first preserved omen is apodosis no. 23, which occurs in omens 8, 9, 17, and 18. In the second omen, only the date of the first invisibility, XII? 24, and that of the next first visibility, XI 28, are preserved. Since a period of invisibility that extends over 11 months 4 days is impossible, the month name read as XII may represent a mistake for X, in which case this omen would be identical to omen 55. Note that omen 55 corresponds to omen 16, but 55 refers to last visibility in the West and 16 to last visibility in the East. A last visibility in the East on XII 25 is recorded in 10 which is a report, not an omen. If the second fragmentary omen in K were to be identified with omen 10, one would have to assume that K substituted the date of Ω in 11 for that of Ξ in 10; one could then reconstruct omens 10 and 11 as follows:

10	Σ XII 25	3m 16d	Ξ III 11	8m 17d	
11	Ω XI 28	17d	Γ XII 15		

None of these solutions seems convincing to us.